MEDITATIONS
for
Psychic
DEVELOPMENT

© Troy Parkinson

ABOUT THE AUTHOR

Chanda Parkinson's diverse background and passions include the arts and music, professional work in the nonprofit sector, owning and operating several businesses, volunteering as a social justice and human rights advocate, and mothering three children. An early life interest in Christian theological studies blossomed and expanded to include Eastern Philosophies tied to Buddhism and Taoism, Metaphysical and Esoteric studies, and Celtic Shamanic Practices, which she continues to devour with great fervor. She has been a student of psychic development for more than twenty years. Chanda has been a professional psychic intuitive, tarot practitioner, esoteric astrologist, and spiritual teacher for more than fifteen years. She holds a tremendous desire to contribute through meaningful work in the world. Her greatest joy is witnessing others discovering and stepping into their own natural spiritual gifts. *Meditations for Psychic Development* is her first published book.

CHANDA PARKINSON

MEDITATIONS
for
Psychic
DEVELOPMENT

PRACTICAL EXERCISES
to awaken your
SIXTH SENSE

LLEWELLYN PUBLICATIONS
Woodbury, Minnesota

FIRST EDITION
First Printing, 2021

Book design by Samantha Peterson
Cover design by Shira Atakpu

Llewellyn Publications is a registered trademark of Llewellyn Worldwide Ltd.

Library of Congress Cataloging-in-Publication Data
Names: Parkinson, Chanda, 1973– author. | Title: Meditations for psychic development : practical exercises to awaken your sixth sense / Chanda Parkinson. Description: First edition. | Woodbury, Minnesota : Llewellyn Publications, 2021. | Includes bibliographical references. | Summary: "Practice-based exercises to increase and/or develop one's psychic abilities"— Provided by publisher.
Identifiers: LCCN 2021013220 (print) | LCCN 2021013221 (ebook) | ISBN 9780738764337 (paperback) | ISBN 9780738764818 (ebook)
Subjects: LCSH: Psychic ability—Problems, exercises, etc.
Classification: LCC BF1031 .P345 2021 (print) | LCC BF1031 (ebook) | DDC 133.8—dc23
LC record available at https://lccn.loc.gov/2021013220
LC ebook record available at https://lccn.loc.gov/2021013221

Llewellyn Worldwide Ltd. does not participate in, endorse, or have any authority or responsibility concerning private business transactions between our authors and the public.
    All mail addressed to the author is forwarded but the publisher cannot, unless specifically instructed by the author, give out an address or phone number.
    Any internet references contained in this work are current at publication time, but the publisher cannot guarantee that a specific location will continue to be maintained. Please refer to the publisher's website for links to authors' websites and other sources.

Llewellyn Publications
A Division of Llewellyn Worldwide Ltd.
2143 Wooddale Drive
Woodbury, MN 55125-2989
www.llewellyn.com

Printed in the United States of America

DEDICATION

This book is dedicated to all the followers of the spirit realm. It takes courage, presence, and discipline to maintain a sense of wonder in a chaotic and demanding world. I honor you with this work. To all of my beautifully talented women blood and bone ancestors who did not get to express themselves freely, I express your voices through my own because you could not. Finally, to my children, who sang my soul awake the moment they were born. No matter the naysayers, stay true to yourself always.

Contents

Acknowledgments

Thank you to my wonderful children Jacob, Addi, and Mia for giving up precious time with me over the months it took me to write this, and for supporting me with your love and ongoing encouragement. My deepest gratitude goes out to my partner, Troy, for carrying more of the weight with our household and children while simultaneously being both my harshest critic and my biggest fan. You have put up with my self-doubt while repeatedly pushing me to stretch out of my own comfort zones. To my dearest friends who listened while I endlessly spoke about this project, you know who you are and I am forever grateful. To my clients over the years: you are the reason this book happened at all. Thank you for inspiring me daily. My greatest joy is seeing you open doors to your own psychic abilities, self-awareness, and the beautiful part you play in making this world a better place. I am perpetually in awe of how gifted you all are, and honored I get to be included on your journeys.

Finally, many thanks to the publishing team at Llewellyn. Your wisdom provided beautiful shape to all the material I presented from the beginning. I am so thankful for your willingness to work with a first-time author.

Foreword

If you've picked up this book, you're about to embark on an exciting, sometimes frustrating, but very rewarding journey. Having an interest in psychic development is a natural part of being human. I remember my own beginnings, which I document in my 2009 book, *Bridge to the Afterlife*.

It was more than twenty years ago, I was going to college in Boston and after two unexpected deaths, I felt a calling to explore all things psychic and mediumship. I read numerous books, attended development circles, and slowly over time, began sharing my gifts as a medium with people from all walks of life.

Over the years, I've learned that one of the best ways to develop your psychic abilities is by implementing a meditation practice. Meditation is an ancient technique that receives a lot of buzz about how to do it, when to do it, why to do it. Ultimately, it is a sacred experience of quieting oneself and expanding one's senses for peace, tranquility, and new insight.

But I'm not going to lie. Meditation isn't easy for me. I still come up with a number of reasons not to do it.

I can't focus.

I can't take the time.

I'm too ... blah, blah, blah.

And yet, I know somewhere deep within me is a sense ... a knowingness, that when I've completed a meditation session, I will have a new level of presence and understanding, and if nothing else, it will bring healing to my physical body and insight to my human experience.

I wish I'd had this book when I started.

Of course, I've read numerous books that teach psychic development and numerous books that teach meditation, but I never found a practical book that blended both of them with clarity, ease, and grace. This book does that. It does so in a down-to-earth, easily digestible way. Each chapter is jam-packed with both excellent information for psychic development and also powerful meditations specifically designed to help you develop your innate awareness today!

It's also written by an extraordinary teacher and mentor. I have been blessed to know Chanda for more than twenty-four years; if I know anything to be true about her character and essence, it's that she is fiercely committed to helping people develop their psychic gifts in a clear, compassionate, and direct way. I often call her a compassionate pit bull. She loves her students with such conviction that she sees right to the heart of where they are going and doesn't sugarcoat what they need to do to get there.

Chanda has committed her life to educating others. She received her master's degree in theatre education from Emerson College. She's designed lesson plans for inner-city schools. She has coached and mentored hundreds of people on their psychic development. Chanda is not a flowery "woo-woo" person. She is a grounded, focused, educator. And because she's been in your shoes, she knows the importance of developing psychic gifts with a solid foundation. These meditations help lay that foundation.

The first time I experienced these meditations I was immediately aware of how powerful they were. They reignited my connection spirit and I found myself grateful for this text because it helped remind me of what I've always felt inside. I am more than this physical body. My spirit is a part of something so much bigger than I can comprehend. And incorporating these meditations into my life connected me to a deep sense of peace that I had forgotten. A peace that is only present when I am authentically connected to my true source.

As you begin this book, I encourage you to follow each of the steps Chanda lays out in the chapters. I encourage you to journal and really commit to taking on this meditation process from start to finish. The gifts you discover on the other side of this practice will be worth it. The best part is this isn't a one-and-done book. These meditations not only build on each other as a whole but each individual meditation offers new insight with each session.

Take a moment. Close your eyes. Breathe in and out. Begin to recognize that inner voice inside of you that is eager to be revealed.

With Love,

Troy Parkinson

Medium, author of *Bridge to the Afterlife*

Introduction

We all have psychic abilities, though how each one of us receives is different. For some it may be through feeling, for others it is a deep inner knowing, and for others it may be hearing or seeing. There is no one-size-fits-all approach to developing your abilities. However, over the years, working with dozens of budding psychics, the one method I have found most effective to open psychic abilities no matter what sort of receiver you are is through meditation.

Meditation is one of the most universal tools for awareness and healing. If you are a beginner to meditation, there is nothing to be intimidated by. All the exercises in this book are asking you to do is calm your mind and focus mental energies on something while discovering all the ways in which you receive psychically and intuitively. There is nothing fancy or complicated about the meditations in this book. With practice and time, you will master them and they will become a regular part of your psychic development rituals.

You are reading this book because you too have a budding interest and fascination in what exists beyond what your five senses can detect alone. You are a seeker. You want information and avenues into your own psychic gifts. If you are an introvert like me, you want a pathway that does not include sitting in a stuffy room listening to a teacher, surrounded by other eager seekers at the edge of their seats. Group psychic development definitely has its benefits. However, you don't need to be in a class or group to develop your own gifts. A meditation practice is a foundation upon which to build your psychic abilities, and it's also highly personal. This book provides an avenue of self-study primarily for beginners.

Developing your psychic abilities is a tremendous form of mind discipline. It greatly strengthens and supports your own inner focus. It is a mind-expanding practice that raises your awareness of your own path and the world around you. It can be a way to replenish your own energy reserves, and afford yourself periodic breaks from the daily grind. It can teach you how to better manage your own energy flow, and to buffer from negative influences around you. It will improve your relationships, as you'll be better in tune with the people around you. It can be a guide to help you solve problems. It is one of the most unselfish acts of love, as it improves your own life and enriches the lives of those around you.

You are about to embark upon a wonderful journey of self-exploration through the development of your psychic abilities through meditation. This book is a twenty-years-long culmination of practices, exercises, knowledge, and wisdom I have incorporated over time in my own life, education, and through the mentoring of others. I didn't know in the beginning of my own meditation practice that long ago that it would serve as a tool for deeper awareness, information, and developing of my own gifts. However, in the process of my own exploration of my gifts, I was able to root myself in meditation as a foundational practice when I lived in a smaller city, with no outside support for development. It was a beautiful discovery, and I decided a long time ago to dedicate a portion of my life's work to assisting others in exploring and opening to their own abilities through meditative practices.

Exercising the meditations in this book will provide a foundation from which to build a connection with your own personal gifts. In addition, you will have a greater understanding of yourself as a psychic receiver. This book provides an opportunity to filter out unnecessary steps to get you to the core of your abilities. The number one barrier to developing one's own abilities is the lack of direction on where to begin. The second barrier is a lack of clarity regarding what a person's specific abilities may be.

The book is broken down into two parts. The first part explores the foundational basics of how you work as a psychic receiver, and it sets the tone for building upon your own abilities. The second part explores various ways in which your own psychic abilities function and bring in information. When you are willing to explore all the areas, you can then begin to establish a framework for working your gifts. You may discover you are a gifted medium but are not able to see auras, for example. You'll get to try both! Or, you may learn that you connect easily with past lives and that your gifts function best when used in nature, but you don't easily feel energy. There are different ways in which psychics frame the messages and information received. I am giving you plenty of options to explore, in order to discover the ways in which you function most optimally as a psychic.

This book aims to assist you in cutting out the guesswork and arriving at the core of your own gifts. However, it's not a process to rush through. Please don't skip the information portions of the chapters to head for the exercises. All the information presented is important to assist you in setting the tone for your own psychic practice. Psychic work is a complex and involved process, and unless you understand some ground rules before you start, it could prove a confusing or even distressing experience. Cover your bases as you go through each chapter.

Now that we have noted what your psychic gifts can do for you, here are some important things that your abilities *cannot* do for you:

- Predict the future with certainty. It can only give probability patterns, because each of us has the willpower over his or her own life to change things. Use your gifts to help yourself and others see and sense the cycles and patterns in life with sharpness, and probable outcomes instead of definitives.

- Provide a fast answer to all life's problems. Life, after all, is meant to be lived, and some things are not meant to be known. Embrace a dual purpose: to know your own humanness, and to experience your own limitlessness as a spirit. If you dedicate time to learning how to narrow the field of possibilities to a particular problem or question, using a combination of sixth-sense insight and intuition, you will achieve accurate results.

- Your abilities are not to be used as entertainment or in harmful ways that hurt others. Being responsible with your developing practice requires great care and attentiveness. Nurture your development and extend that same nurturing to others. Keep your heart centered, and your purpose grounded in service.

- Finally, changing others. Your gifts, no matter how powerful they are, aren't meant to be used to change other people. You may use your own particular sensitivities to understand someone else's behaviors and actions, or how to handle certain interpersonal situations, but you are not here to change them.

After covering important foundational basics in the first chapters of this book, you will have the opportunity to learn how to connect with spiritual guides, loved ones, your higher self, animal spirits, past lives, and more. Much like exercise benefits the physical body, the more you practice these psychic development meditations and work to deepen the connections, the stronger your psychic muscle becomes. I am providing an avenue in this book for beginning seekers. You need no previous experience in psychic development to use the meditations in this book. It's meant to be a foundational resource, one that you can come back to repeatedly.

I suggest making the most of this book by recording your own voice reading the meditations and then listening and journaling at the end of each chapter. Recording your own voice reading the meditations has its advantages: you'll be able to keep them on hand for times when you would like to repeat the chapters and meditations, allowing you to easily repeat the meditations in this book multiple times. Once you've completed this meditative study, you'll naturally feel drawn to some of the meditations more than others. I know I have my favorites, and you will too.

At the end of each chapter you will see tips for use and a section for journaling. I cannot emphasize enough how important regular documentation (journaling) of your own psychic experiences is, whether those experiences are intentional or random. Journaling is a simple tool for continued reflection and further understanding of your own gifts. Plus it's a fun and creative way to tell the stories of the wonderful things you will be experiencing along this journey.

The best tip for writing in your journal is to do it frequently and to refrain from editing your experiences. Something that might seem insignificant to you may later turn out to be important guidance. A psychic journal validates the process of developing over time. You learn quickly what your strongest gifts are through the process of documentation. Psychic development is one part practice, one part recording, and one part reflection. Over time you begin to see patterns and themes in what comes through you via your gifts. Use this log of your experiences to assist your growth personally and psychically. All you need is ten minutes a day.

There really aren't limits to the use of your psychic journal. For example, we all have déjà vu experiences. Write them down. Synchronicities, repetitive number patterns, knowing something before it happens, receiving spontaneous words of guidance, and feeling the presence of loved ones are all wonderful moments to capture for later reference. When life gets busy and you aren't able to spend time in psychic development, you can always go back to your journal as a guidepost; re-reading your entries may motivate you to continue exploring.

Some of the meditations will draw you in much more strongly than others. However, if you do these exercises consistently from beginning to end, you will see results. This book was designed to be used from beginning to end, after which you can revisit and pluck out the exercises that seem to resonate with you the most for repetitive use. Using this book as a guide will help you measure your own progress.

I want you to feel as though you are free to experiment without the watching eyes and judgment from others, without unnecessary guidelines and tests, without pressure to perform in any one particular way, and to have a method for going at your own pace. Even with the step-by-step actions presented here, you will still need to pay attention to how you are feeling about this work. If you are struggling, take a break. Where you feel the most inspired, continue. Adjust, adapt, and note the cues and signals your own gifts are offering you. Above all, refrain from overanalyzing everything. The quickest way to sabotage your practice is to overthink the experiences you are having.

The deceased mother of one of my clients visited my client in a meditation. She reached out to me in a moment of frustration, wondering why she contacted her and what she was trying to say. I replied that what she was trying to say was irrelevant—the most important thing was that her mother was making contact.

If there was anything to know, she would know it. We don't get to control the outcome of what we receive. Receptivity must be in a space of openness. Then we let the messages or impressions simmer, step back, and rest in the joy of the connection until next time.

This book will lead you toward a psychic practice that demands trust and faith in the process. You'll be a happier psychic with minimal need for perfection. Keep your own expectations in check. Enjoy the ride.

ONE

The Power of Meditation

You are about to embark upon a journey of psychic development through meditation. Before you begin making your way through the chapters and meditations presented here, stop for a moment and ask yourself these important questions: What do you perceive as the purpose of meditation in your life? What previous expectations have you held about what meditation is?

Meditation is any practice undertaken for the purpose of quieting the mind. Through quieting the mind, we open ourselves to a more relaxed state, where further healing benefits, insights, calm, and bliss can occur. Science has widely researched and documented the positive effect on things such as sleep, blood pressure, and mood. Here we take it a step further, exploring how meditation serves as a tool for expanded awareness and psychic skills development.

Mindfulness meditation not only serves the purpose of calm and relaxation. It also disciplines the senses to observe and receive what comes in through the environment and your own sixth sense. It is at the point in which you are in your most relaxed, calm state that you are more apt to receive important information for your own life path, visions, words, feelings, and supportive healing energies for yourself and others.

Meditation is one of the oldest, easiest, most calming strategies for welcoming a wide range of insights and information. To begin a meditation practice, all you need is a quiet, calm place to relax and be silent. This can be indoors or outdoors, as long as you know you won't be disrupted. I have clients who meditate on their lunch breaks at work. They close the door, turn off their phone, and go to a deep place of calm. There is nothing fancy needed to craft a successful meditation practice.

Next, think of where your body is the most comfortable. Is there a room in your home that instantly calms you? Perhaps there are soft cushions on a corner chair that relax your body. Go there. Do you fall asleep easily? You may wish to sit up instead of lying down. Do your senses respond to relaxing scents? Perhaps try diffusing some lavender essential oil in your space. The key to a successful meditation practice is to choose a format you can rely upon consistently. Use your imagination to create it. I love having my large rose quartz crystal from South Africa nearby when I meditate. It instantly calms me when I gaze upon it. If you enjoy using technology, download some soft music or apps for guided meditations. This is a wonderful way to practice getting comfortable with meditation in general.

My body responds to relaxation techniques that are pleasing to the senses, so I am all about the soft music, lighting candles, sitting somewhere warm and comfortable, and in a beautiful space. There are no limits to the things you can add to your own meditation practice. My advice is to choose something that resonates and keep it simple. Too many steps add complication and distraction. If you don't want the burden of a ritual, you can also choose to be silent in a quiet, dark room. You may also try taking a walk or watching a sunset. Or mix it up, and try some of each!

There are steps I recommend as a foundational basis to grow upon. I encourage each meditation to begin with breath. To slow down the body and the mind through slowing the breath produces the optimal atmosphere for insights to be received. Next, it is important to ground and center for protection. Why not be free to explore, as long as you stay connected to your body and this planet? It can feel disorienting to go deeply into meditation without grounding, so practice that regularly.

Moving into meditation with intention also feels important. Going in with a question, concern, or something you are intending to receive as guidance or for understanding will make these meditations far more productive. If you aren't interested in asking a question, then simply going in with the intention to feel more relaxed and calm is still an intention. It will add form and shape to the experience rather than leaving you feeling confused with the outcome if nothing happens.

Here is what will happen with diligent attention to your psychic meditation practice. You will ultimately blossom further your own deep well of empathy, compassion, and unconditional love. That in itself is a tremendous gift. The power of this space moves you out of your own thinking mind to a greater awareness of yourself as a spirit, connected in a state of oneness with all other spirits and to humankind. It has the added benefit of producing insights for your own life path, something I call the warm milk and honey moment. It's the delicious additional benefit of cultivating a meditation practice. Wisdom can surface from out of nowhere about yourself and others. Over time, you become alert to the patterns and cycles in your personal life, relationships, career path, and spiritual journey. You learn to shift and adjust to meet the demands and rigors of daily life without feeling as though you are running on empty. You recharge your batteries; you increase your own vibrational energy. You know the next steps, as if you had just consulted a wise master.

You'll know that you are receiving information, insights, and messages through your psychic gifts when you feel sudden bursts of motivation or a lightning bolt "a-ha!" moment with surges of positive energy coursing through your mind, heart, and body and a renewed sense of hope and optimism. In other words, it will feel good when your psychic abilities are offering you information and insights. What intuitively feels "off" when you are trying to make a choice will be supported by your psychic abilities, helping you determine the best next step. Things that are of your imagination don't lend the same "zing" of energy through your body, and tend to play with your mind in negative ways. Stay alert throughout the process and you'll easily begin to detect the difference.

As mentioned before, the most important thing for beginners to do is keep a psychic development journal. Even the most minor flashes of insight can be meaningful down the road; don't let those disappear without writing them down.

Here are a few tips on journaling from your own psychic experiences:

- Write the current date at the top of the page.
- Describe in detail the information, symbols, and feelings you received.
- Reflect on your current life and connect the dots with what you received.
- If you can't make sense of something in the present moment, put it away. Trust that in time, you'll know why you received what you did.
- Write down what the information made you feel and think about.
- Record any further questions this brought to your mind for later reflection.

Meditative practices make your life better, with the added benefit of grounding you in service to the world. Meditation not only assists us in growing our psychic abilities, it also lets us experience the rich awareness of engaging in and contributing to humanity, helps us figure out the steps to following our dreams, and supports us in creating a more joyful existence. The guided meditations in this book will expand your psychic gifts and also serve as a foundational starting point for directing your own life and actions in service to the world. It is through spiritual and meditative practices that we become stronger, improve our spiritual armor, and gain the ability to extend our reach beyond the four walls of our home.

Each person will get something different from this book. You and I are both psychic, but we do not receive in the same ways. Discovering the ways in which you receive through your own innate psychic gifts can be exhilarating, at times confusing, fulfilling, and eye-opening. This discovery offers you another lens through which to know yourself more deeply. You do not need to spend hours each day to do so, and actually I do not recommend that much time; ten to twenty minutes of practice daily or every other day is more than sufficient to feel more harmonized with yourself, your life and choices, and the world.

Know that much of the world of psychic development requires a healthy level of exploration and experimentation as well as an ability to trust in the process. Gifts and abilities open differently for everyone. There will be times that a flurry of information or symbols crowds your inner vision or your inner knowing blossoms suddenly and you may not make sense of it immediately. All of this is perfectly normal. As you progress, you will start to see familiar patterns in how you receive information. They will act as codes that help you decipher the meaning behind the messages. How inspiring to consider that through entering a space of regular deep quiet and meditation, you can also access important information to assist yourself and others. This process unfolds one step at a time.

Blessings on your journey! I am excited for what you are about to embark on. My deepest wish for you is that you begin to discover your own gifts, and are motivated and inspired to continue on your own path of development. Allow these meditations to ignite your desire to deepen innate abilities. I believe you were called to this book. May it serve as a beacon of hope, lifting you to the heights of greater awareness.

The next chapters determine what type of psychic receiver you are, known as the four "clairs": clairvoyant, clairsentient, clairaudient, and claircognizant.

FOR YOUR JOURNAL

What three things will you use from the list for your meditation ritual? What are your goals for your meditation practice?

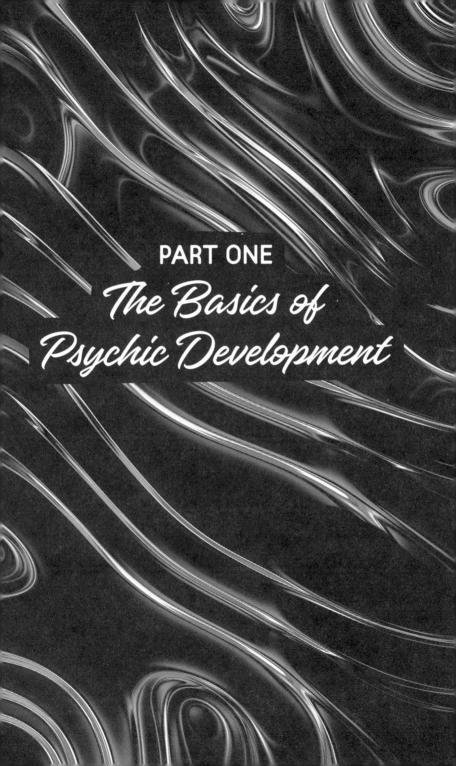

PART ONE
The Basics of Psychic Development

TWO
The Clairs

The word *psychic* is Greek in origin and means "of the soul." Developing your own psychic abilities allows you the awareness of the true nature of your soul. Exercising your psychic abilities is like providing your soul with a lighthouse in the midst of the rocky and sometimes uncertain seas of life. Where once the ship's destination was hidden by fog, the lighthouse suddenly pierces through, steering a more direct course to shore. Your abilities shine the light to bring what is needed: perhaps a message, a nugget of wisdom, a vision for next steps, symbols, an inner knowing, or validation for an important decision. By developing your own psychic abilities, you gift yourself the chance to understand important guideposts and cues around you. In addition, using your psychic gifts to connect with another at a soul level can contribute tremendous insights and healing. It is an enriching practice that benefits all.

The word "psychic" is the broad term that represents so many different types of abilities, not one particular set. Just like the word "doctor" represents many different specialties, so can the word "psychic" be used to represent many different sensitivities and gifts. Depending on what type of receiver you are, psychics can see, feel, hear, sense, and know, or some of the combination of all of those.

We will begin with what are commonly known as the "clairs," the spiritual mechanisms through which everyone is designed to receive. While it is true there are many more, for the sake of covering the basics, we will stick to the four primary clairs: clairvoyance (clear seeing), clairsentience (clear feeling), clairaudience (clear hearing), and claircognizance (clear knowing). Knowing which of the clairs represent your abilities will allow you to use your time spent in development appropriately.

Once you know which kind of psychic receiver you are, you will have direction and focus for your own psychic practice. In order to more consciously use your psychic abilities, you must clear out the beliefs and ideas that keep you from knowing and receiving your spiritual truth. This is a process of remembering, so to speak, your inherent ability. You don't have to learn to become psychic—you already are that. Psychic development through meditation will bring you closer to your own strengths and most natural functioning as a psychic.

Take out your journal. What follows is a simple list of questions to answer in order:

1. As a learner, are you supported with visual aids?

2. Do you play out life scenarios and scenes in your mind's eye on a regular basis? Do you have an active imagination?

3. Do you ever wake up in the middle of the night with an idea and often can't go back to sleep unless you get up and write it down?

4. Do you ever wake in the middle of the night with a gut feeling that something is going to happen to you or to someone else but you don't always know what it is?

5. Do you easily feel the emotions of those around you?

6. Do large crowds and busy public spaces overwhelm you?

7. Do you like to write? Or are you good at putting words together to describe or explain things?

8. When others are speaking about their problems, do you hear words in your head that are often solutions?

9. Do you ever have an experience where it's as if someone else is speaking in your head?

10. Do you ever just know something without really knowing how you know and it turns out to be true?

11. Would you say you often follow your gut intuition successfully?

12. Do you consider yourself a quick decision maker and problem solver?

If you said yes to questions 1 through 3, you likely receive through your third eye, or inner vision and are clairvoyant. If you said yes to questions 4 through 6, you consider yourself sensitive and tuned in to emotional undercurrents of energy and are clairsentient. If you said yes to questions 7 through 9, you are able to hear and channel into the form of words and so are clairaudient. And if you said yes to questions 10 through 12, your sense of inner knowing is strong and you are claircognizant.

Psychics who are primarily clairvoyant are mediums, seers, and tarot readers. Psychics who are clairsentient are body healers and empaths. Psychics who are clairaudient are the channelers, speakers, and spirit writers; those who are claircognizant are intuitives and spiritual teachers, as well as counselors and guides. It is fun to begin to see already where you naturally fit within the various different psychic categories. You are likely more than one type, and it's definitely possible to be all of them. Choose one or two that you would like to develop first and expand from there.

TOOLS

You can also learn more about your potential as a psychic through the lens of your own sun sign. Of course, your sign is only one small part of your entire astrology blueprint; however, it can grant you a sneak peek into your psychic potential and the manner in which you receive. An esoteric astrologer can help you learn more about the whole of your spiritual abilities based on your chart.

The water signs—Cancer, Scorpio, and Pisces—are the most naturally psychic. The water element is associated with emotion and intuition, a pretty powerful combo for these extremely sensitive signs. These multi-talented zodiac signs can master many aspects of the psychic and healing arts and put them together in combination for powerful healing experiences.

The fire signs—Aries, Leo, and Sagittarius—often receive through swift flashes of insight and spurts of channeled creativity and ideas. These signs are often naturally gifted teachers and speakers. They absorb and easily share information whether in their surroundings or from beyond. You will often find this element drawn to ways in which we may explore outside our ordinary reality. Psychedelics, breathwork, and physical tests of inner stamina (such as periodic fasting) can all be ways in which to tap powerful cosmic awareness for these signs.

The air signs—Gemini, Libra, and Aquarius—receive through listening. It's common for them to hear voices and be highly communicative, and their intuition can operate in short bursts. These are the gifted channelers, advisers, teachers, and guides. Automatic writing and tarot cards are wonderful tools for air signs, as they make swift connections between ideas, pictures, concepts, and information.

The earth signs—Taurus, Virgo, and Capricorn—receive impressions through their five senses: tasting, touching, hearing, smelling, and seeing. They are the most naturally grounded psychics. They often have kinesthetic sensibilities that make them wonderful hands-on healers and medical intuitives, as they can be quite sensitive to the physical body. Earth-based spiritual practices such as shamanism is often a subject earth signs find very interesting.

No matter your sign, this undertaking is an exciting one. It is so joyful and rewarding when you begin to put the puzzle pieces of your own abilities together. I became interested in the psychic arts as far back as 1998, when I was first introduced to mediumship and spiritualism. However, my own psychic development didn't really take off until after someone read my tarot cards at a party. It astounded me how she could know that much about my inner world, just from looking at pictures on a few cards. It was so powerful that I went to get my own tarot deck the next day. That defining moment sparked my own path of learning and discovery. I devoured the knowledge and wisdom of the tarot. Twenty years later, I still credit that night as a major turning point for my own soul's path. In that moment, I knew I was going to read tarot cards. Follow your own impulses. Where you feel led to explore is probably the best next step.

FOR YOUR JOURNAL

After taking the quiz, which one or two of the clairs was the strongest for you? Why? Can you recall a time when you used your clair gift either intentionally or unintentionally? Describe where you were and what happened to confirm your insight to the best of your ability. What does your zodiac sign and element tell you about how you receive?

THREE

Clairvoyance Meditation

The gift of clairvoyance, or clear vision, is an extrasensory perception that allows you to perceive, within the mind's eye, symbols or images for yourself or for someone else. The messages (which can pertain to the past, the present, or the potential future) come forward through symbols or mental images reflected in a similar way to a distant memory or a slide show on the inner or third eye, without the help of the physical eyes. Your third eye is the space that holds your inner vision, right around the area of the pituitary gland, between your eyebrows and about a quarter-inch back. The impressions are more easily perceived through the deeply relaxed space of meditation.

Clairvoyant visions often come in as metaphors for current life situations, as the appearance of dramatic scenes or as psychic symbols that together reveal important messages. If you are experiencing a heightened level of emotion after a devastating breakup, you may be shown ocean waves crashing on a rocky shore, for instance. Your inner vision may show the birth of a baby that is unrelated to actual birth; instead, it is a beautiful vision that represents new beginnings. Or perhaps you are undergoing a meaningful transition from one major phase of life to the next and are shown a butterfly emerging from a cocoon or a snake shedding its skin. What will come to you is highly unpredictable, and you may not know what those symbols mean at first, which is a completely normal part of the process of establishing your own personal code.

As a clairvoyant, you must develop a strategy for when you happen to see something alarming. I have had clients who have had visions of something negative happening to family members, for example, or natural disasters that have not yet happened. While this gift is incredibly powerful, in these instances there is usually nothing that can be done to avoid or prevent those experiences from happening, and they cause unnecessary fear and disruption. You can stop disruptive insights by visualizing a beautiful flower blossom gently closing its petals over your third eye, located in the middle of your forehead. In addition, breathing exercises for grounding and releasing the energy in those visions is also helpful. Many years ago I made a pact with my own spiritual team on the other side that I only wanted to see what was helpful and supportive in people's lives, not what may cause others fear. Be clear about your intentions as you move into this work; it will keep your mind and visions clear of what you no longer wish to see.

Over time, you will become comfortable with how your inner vision works, the repetitive nature of the impressions, and the messages they hold. In the beginning it's comforting to remind yourself that those visions are often less likely actual events playing out and more a story describing the tone, atmosphere, or nature of what is happening. Knowing your astrological sun sign can also help you realize the mechanism through which you most easily receive.

CLAIRVOYANCE AND THE ZODIAC

In these initial chapters, four signs of the zodiac are broken down to highlight the way in which each sign is largely influenced by each of the clairs. That said, you can be another sign in the zodiac not listed and still be clairvoyant, for example. You are likely more than one clair all at once; that is what makes you unique! No two people receive the same way. Allow the information here to provide a starting point or a way to think about your own abilities.

Sagittarius: This sign receives far-sighted vision, hints of future potential, and is the most prophetic of the zodiac.

Pisces: The most psychic sign. Although Pisces can access and receive with most of the clairs, the strongest for them is to sense past, present, and future potential through visions. People of this sign make remarkable mediums and psychic healers.

Scorpio: As gifted mediums, this sign has the potential to easily pierce the veil and see, connect, and communicate with spirits.

Capricorn: Having a clear sense of the past, present, and future potential alongside the ability to ground insights into reality, this sign receives tremendous practical, down-to-earth visions.

TOOLS

Clairvoyants see spirits of loved ones on their inner vision, or connect with important messages through dreams. They can receive spontaneous insights about past lives or connect with visual cues from their environment rich in messages and clues. Learning to activate your third eye will continue to assist you in expanding this already natural gift.

The encouragement in strengthening your own clairvoyant ability is to allow yourself to honor what you see first. Trusting your first impressions is important; they often arrive and leave quickly. It will not serve you to try to analyze or find the logic in what you receive during this meditation. Save any additional analysis for your journaling afterward.

MEDITATION

Either sit or lie down; either will work for this meditation. Use your breath to ground you. Feel safe, at ease, and ready to access and open your own clairvoyant vision.

Notice that your breathing has now slowed to an even, natural pace. You are beginning to soften and relax. You are focused on your breathing, and now bring all of your attention to your third eye, right between your eyebrows in the middle of your forehead. This inner viewing screen is where your gift of clairvoyance is realized.

Take all the time you need to feel a deeply relaxed pace of breathing with each breath. Begin to notice any sensations in your third eye as it begins to shift—any tingling, pressure, numbness, or pulsing energy.

With your eyes closed, place your focus on your third eye and see the number 1 in your inner vision. Hold your attention there until you see the number with your mind's eye. Then replace it with the number 2, and then the number 3, and so on until you reach the number 12. When you have successfully seen these numbers using your inner eye, you may move on to the next step.

Use your inner vision now to go to your own personal sanctuary in nature. This is the place where you go to escape the physical world around you. See yourself in your mind's eye walking around your sanctuary. Look down at the ground and notice what's under your feet. Allow yourself to take a full minute to just orientate yourself to where you are standing before moving on.

With each relaxed breath you take now, feel yourself easing into the natural surroundings. Notice an inner eagerness to explore growing within you. Breathe and relax even more peacefully into this place. Feel the good intentions of this beautiful landscape assisting you with your own inner journey of opening your psychic gifts.

Allow your inner vision to magnify the colors of your surroundings. The blues are brilliant and deep; the rich hues of green in the vegetation around you are startling. You see every outline and detail with more and more clarity the longer you are in this space. Walk around for a full minute just to look at your surroundings.

An object catches your attention, and out of curiosity you move toward it. Examine the specks of varied color in the object. Notice the shape, the size, and anything about this object that makes it unique. If it helps, say out loud what you are seeing, as if you are describing the object to someone else. Elaborate as long as you wish, as it can take you deeper into your surroundings.

You are now drawn deeper into your sanctuary where you happen upon a flower bud. It is a brilliant indigo color, and as you gaze upon it, it begins to glow. This flower is a symbol for the blossoming of your own inner vision. You take several beats to be with the unopened bud of this flower. Suddenly the petals gently and slowly begin to open. As they do so, you feel your own inner vision opening.

In an instant, you feel suddenly lifted off the ground as the ground you are standing on raises you up above your surroundings. Suddenly you find yourself lifted into the clouds, where you are swept away and carried through the sky. As you gaze down, you are able to crystallize more of your surroundings in your mind's eye.

Without a moment's pause, you are surrounded by a rainbow. You reach your hands out and the colors seem to connect with your hands and body, one at a time, washing over you like a cleansing rainbow of healing light. Red, orange, yellow, green, blue, and purple all surge in a beautiful stream through your hands up through your arms and body. You feel renewed and restored.

The cloud slowly lowers you down to the ground now. You find yourself at the mouth of a cave. For your convenience, a lantern has been provided so you may walk in and explore. Feel yourself becoming eager to see what is waiting for you inside. As you walk along, you slow down and glance at the walls of the cave. Impressions and indentations carved there suddenly become symbols, pictures, and images that form swiftly before you. Some may tell a story, others may seem random with no apparent connection.

At the end of the path you see a stone table with a wooden box on top. Out of curiosity, you go to the box. On the side of the box are written the words "inside lies what you need to see to assist you on your life's path." You carefully lift the lid, and inside is a gift just for you. It may be words of wisdom, it may be an object that has significance to you, or it may be a clue for what it is you need to do next. Trust your first impression. Close the box. Now it is time to go back to where you came from.

You walk with a greater sense of confidence now, through the cave to your sanctuary in nature, bringing with you what it is you need to help you. Send out your gratitude to this place as you walk along the path. Feel yourself now coming back into your body, having learned what it is you needed for this moment in time. Take a few nice, deep breaths. Through your grounding cords, release whatever you no longer wish to keep as part of your journey.

Open your eyes and prepare to write in your journal.

Helpful Guidance: In the beginning, I recommend practicing mostly with your eyes closed. Eventually you'll want to try doing the meditation with eyes open to see if you can get similar information. Above all, your third eye will still reflect no matter if your eyes are open or closed. You may also choose to place a clear quartz crystal over your third eye when you are lying down to assist in the opening of your clairvoyant vision.

FOR YOUR JOURNAL

What symbols, images, impressions, or scenes played out during the meditation? Recap as many of the details as you can for interpretation. Make use of any books or online resources to assist in the understanding of the object or gift you were given.

FOUR

Clairsentience Meditation

Those who consider themselves the most sensitive physically and emotionally experience the gift of clairsentience, clear feeling. Information is received through the body and heart, usually experienced as a flash of emotion, the same sensations as someone struggling with a health issue, or flashes of insight about someone's physical body when hands are laid on another person. Clairsentient people are the most empathic, sensitive souls among us. This is also the most common of the psychic abilities.

When you grow your gift of clairsentience, you can easily navigate the world of cluttered energy all around us. Take time to notice your mood swings or unaccountable changes of feeling. Who were you just with? Where were you? Pay attention to how crowded places make you feel. Practice asking questions of your intuition and see how responses come to you. And listen to how you speak. If you often talk about feeling "into" something, or feeling the "vibe" of a person or thing, your own language is pointing out your psychic ability.

CLAIRSENTIENCE AND THE ZODIAC

Taurus: Strongly attuned to the five senses, this sign receives through kinesthetic abilities; they feel impressions in their physical bodies and make grounded, wise leaders, philosophers, and guides for others.

Cancer: There is nothing this sign does not feel, and feel it with intensity. These people are empathetic and highly intuitive. It can be difficult sometimes to know which emotions are theirs and which belong to someone else. For this sign, good emotional boundaries are important.

Virgo: People of this sign receive strong impressions in their physical bodies, most commonly as indications of their environment's safety. This sign also easily senses the presence of spirits. Virgos make wonderful hands-on body healers and can assist others in releasing trapped emotions.

If you are not a Taurus, Cancer, or Virgo, you may also be an empath, which isn't sign-specific. Empaths are a type of clairsentient who are often naturally drawn to healing arts such as massage therapy, essential oils, Reiki, or Healing Touch. There is a tremendous capability for high levels of emotional intelligence. Clairsentients must learn good, strong emotional boundaries with others in their lives.

CONSIDER THIS

It is possible to achieve a state known as empathy fatigue, which is a feeling of being a bit overwhelmed with a tremendous sense of compassion and empathy to the point of feeling drained and burned out. It's easy for this to happen, especially in our tremendously tumultuous, changing, and unpredictable world. It can be incredibly triggering for those gifted with clairsentience to see too much of the damaging, violent, and harmful things happening in the news. It's okay to build in a buffer to incoming information from time to time; it can give the senses a much-needed break.

There is a spectrum for determining how empathic you are. Not everyone has the same level of sensitivity. Knowing that you are someone who experiences empathy fatigue, it is wise to give yourself plenty of options for release to stop the overwhelm. My top favorite ways to stop the spin are: heading into nature, to sit calmly, breathe, and reflect. Exercise reduces the level of stress hormones in the body. Talk things out with a trusted friend; get in a body of water or warm bath with your favorite essential oils. I love lavender for its calming properties, but there are several that work quite well to restore a more even, peaceful flow.

TOOLS

Many of my clairsentient clients find themselves happier and feeling more free when they spend time opening their hearts on a regular basis. Enhancing the powers of compassion and opening the heart does exactly what we want it to: allows us to feel emotion without getting swallowed up by the emotion. It can more readily facilitate and inspire action into moments of service and feelings of well-being and bliss.

It is a myth that closing down and protecting your heart keeps you from feeling all the negativity in the world. You know how it feels when something constricts rather than being free to open and flow. When we are afraid of feeling things, we close down and tighten things, and it produces exactly the opposite effect. What this does instead is generate a false sense of safety, and disconnects you from your natural abilities. Learning to keep your heart open while grounding and protecting on a regular basis keeps you in the positive flow as an empath. When you endeavor to walk through life with an open heart, you afford yourself the opportunity to be where your natural gifts are most needed. Keeping your heart open allows you to walk forward, facing the intensity of the world with the strength of your compassionate heart fully intact.

You do not need to be afraid of your own empathic, sensitive, feeling nature. Being empathic and clairsentient doesn't mean you need to hide away from the world. Knowing that you have a home environment you can escape to can be quite comforting, but don't let yourself get stuck there. Just like any other gift, it's the learning process of how to direct it properly that makes you stronger. This is as powerful a gift as all the rest; when harnessed, it can provide a tremendous understanding of life situations you or others are going through.

In addition, clairsentients can be extra sensitive to the physical ailments of themselves and others. This sensitivity comes in handy for knowing your own body. A simple strategy for dissolving the physical sensations of unsure origin is to ask your-self a simple question—"Is this mine or someone else's?"—while breathing and releasing down your grounding cords anything your body is feeling that could have been picked up from some-one else. What isn't yours will leave your body.

One simple activity for developing the gift of clairsentience further is through psychometry, or the reading of energy of objects. Have a friend or family member give you an object that belongs to someone else. Hold it while meditating for five to ten minutes. Take in any feelings, impressions, and information that you receive to relay to the person who gave you the object for verification.

MEDITATION

In a seated position with your feet on the ground, you just feel yourself breathing. Give your full attention to your breath now. Don't focus your attention on breathing; instead, just let your breath happen. Feel the gentle and gradual rise and fall of your chest. Breathe in through your nose and exhale through your mouth. Meet this moment with grace in an upright, comfort-able posture.

This meditation is about being. Begin by centering yourself in your own breath and simply allowing yourself to drop into being. As you now slow down your thoughts and quiet your mind, you go to a place beyond thinking, where you connect with some-thing much bigger than your logical mind can perceive.

Thoughts may enter your mind. Notice them. Honor them. They are a part of you. Thinking is a natural part of being human.

Your thoughts are part of the meditation process. When they come up, simply acknowledge and say goodbye to them, just for now. Make an agreement with your mind that you will come back to any and all thoughts that are important after you finish with your meditation. Allow the ebb and flow of thoughts to come and then go, come and go.

You now begin to feel your own sense of heightened awareness. You feel your skin. You feel the weight of your own body rooting you to the earth. There are many dimensions of your being, and you are now becoming aligned with that dimension in which there is no time. You are becoming aware of the space within where there is stillness, and where it is safe to release all thought. Your thoughts don't leave you forever. You can come back to them at the end of this meditation and pick up where you left off.

When you are ready, become aware of and notice your entire body. Are there areas of stiffness or pain? Release them now. Travel to each area of your body with your awareness. Starting at your feet, relax this area. Now focus on your legs and relax. Move to your mid-section. Release tension from this area of your body. Next, give attention to your arms, shoulders, hands, head, and neck. If there is tension anywhere, recognize it and find ease and comfort in that area, as the tension or soreness melts away. Briefly ask yourself now if you are holding onto anything that belongs to someone else. Breathe and feel the release of what is not yours, what no longer serves you.

Feel the presence of a vibrant glowing rose out in front of you, suspended in space. Let any tension, pain, or stress go to the glowing rose. Send the rose up and out of your space and let it return to where it needs to. You might also see some of these spots of tension and stress float out of your body and down your grounding cord.

Now place all of your attention in your second chakra, your navel, right around the area of your belly button. This space is the center of your clairsentient ability. Here is the space you begin to strengthen, unravel, and become in tune with your own clear feeling abilities. This chakra is directly connected to your emotions and feelings. It is the color orange and spins like an orb. See this vibrant orange orb of energy spinning with momentum now. It is alive and well. As you begin to work with this chakra more and more, in time, you will begin to feel it. You might actually feel it now. What are the sensations? Continue to tune in to this chakra and let your attention be present in this space for a few moments.

Clairsentience can present itself in sensations in the body such as warmth or a vibrating or tingling feeling. It can also cause parts of your body to twitch or tingle, develop a pulse, or another form of awareness of movement inside your belly.

This ability may also present outside your body, in the form of an itch or a poke on your skin. It can also present in feelings of emotion such as happiness or sadness. A gut feeling you have may also be your clairsentience coming forward.

Be aware in the moment of any emotions bubbling up inside your body. Leave any analysis for later; now is not the time to wonder about what you are experiencing. Discipline yourself to stay focused in the moment, and just release the need to know what and why you are feeling what you are. Pay particular attention to the temperature of your body. Is there a hot or a cold spot anywhere?

Sensations commonly associated with clairsentience include chills or goose bumps. If you feel an itch or perhaps as though your limbs are floating, this is your gift awakening. Just notice it and do not be alarmed. You may even feel numbness in other areas of your body or as if someone just placed a warm blanket on your shoulders. This can often be coming from a spirit guide or loved one coming close. These are all validation your senses are opening.

Be present with all these unique sensations of feeling outside of your body for several minutes as they reveal themselves to you fully. There is no need to rush this along.

What are the emotions you are feeling, if any? Are you feeling elation? Happiness? Anticipation and anxiousness? Curiosity? Certainty? Bliss? Is there anything in particular that might be linked to that emotion in the moment? Be neutral now; just observe and feel—don't own the emotions. What if your emotion was suddenly transformed to a color? What would the color be? Is there more than one color?

Be present with each of these unique emotions for several minutes as they surge through your body.

As you begin to become more aware of and in tune with your clairsentience, it awakens. Trust, intend, and expect this ability to strengthen. Even after this meditation is over, your gift continues to blossom.

Now, say to yourself silently or out loud: "I am a spiritual being first and foremost, having a human experience. I have access to my heightened senses at all times. My clairsentience is opening fully. I am feeling the messages I am meant to today."

Be with this certainty for a few moments.

It is time to end this meditation for today. Take a few more deep breaths, release down your grounding cords anything that needs releasing, and allow yourself to slowly move your hands, fingers, and toes. Feel more connected and back in your body. Open your eyes and be ready to move on into the journaling exercise.

Helpful Guidance: What symbols, images, impressions, or scenes played out during the meditation? Record as many of the details as you can for interpretation.

FOR YOUR JOURNAL

What feelings or physical sensations did you experience during the meditation? Record as many of the details as you can for later reflection.

FIVE

Clairaudience Meditation

The gift of clairaudience, or clear hearing, is experienced by those who are the most verbal and communicative. Those with this gift are lovers of words and may be comfortable writing, speaking, teaching, and communicating with others. These people are often the most talkative and typically aren't without opinions, thoughts, and ideas in conversation. In the psychic world, people who are clairaudient make the best channelers. Most psychic mediums work within the clairvoyant and clairaudient realms. The encouragement to grow your gift of clairaudience is to be able to receive messages of guidance and support through your own inner hearing.

The messages that come through clairaudience are straightforward, calm, and direct. I have clients who have experienced everything from being woken because someone was calling their name only to wake up and no one was there, to sitting in meditation and hearing a voice that had a foreign accent, to being in an emergency situation and suddenly being given help-ful direction, to hearing messages from loved ones who have crossed over.

CLAIRAUDIENCE AND THE ZODIAC

Gemini: This sign has the ability to tune in to and channel voices from beyond, thoughts and vibes from others around them, easily crossing the veil to connect with spiritual guides and messages. This is one of the most versatile signs.

Libra: Having an innate sense of how to connect with, communicate, and relate to people, Libras instinctively sense the needs of others, and are the strongest intuitive problem solvers. They are often intuitive word masters who seem to know just the right things to say. Libras know how to read people, period.

Clairaudients are the world's musicians, lyricists, writers, and teachers. They hear voices in surprising ways from out of the blue that tell them how to handle a situation. Clairaudients hear messages from spiritual guides and angels, can hear the laughter of loved ones who have crossed over, hear the wise words of a mentor long since passed away, and are comfortable in the realm of thoughts and words. There is little clairaudients haven't thought of, so don't cross them—they can be the harsh-est critics and are rarely without an opinion.

You may have these qualities and yet aren't one of the two signs listed. Again, this is a simplistic way to evaluate your own potential as a psychic receiver. Other signs may also be clairaudient.

TOOLS

The art of automatic writing is a great way to access clear hearing. The process takes trust and faith, but if it is one of your gifts, you'll find it to be amazingly helpful. Take a half hour or so with your journal in a quiet space where you won't be disturbed. Ask your higher self a question and simply let your pen start writing. It may feel fake or silly at first, but it's important that you don't think about the answer to the question. Instead, let your mind wander and drop into a meditative state. Your pen will start to move, and while you may observe the words as they flow through your mind, you won't be creating them. The difference is subtle, so try it and see.

Pay particular attention now to your surroundings. Be sure to turn off all electrical devices. You may even choose to unplug appliances to block out any noise or disturbances. If you hear a ticking clock, remove it from the room. Create a space free of as many noise disturbances as possible. If you hear traffic, it may be wise to use earplugs or headphones to block out potential disturbances. Prepare yourself for what comes after the meditation: place your journal or a notebook next to you, and hold your pen or pencil in your hand, ready to write.

This meditation in particular is best done without background music. The deeper into silence you are able to go, the more powerful the results.

MEDITATION

Close your eyes and allow your breath to transport you to the sea of calm in your mind and body. Your mind is easily releasing the need to hold onto thoughts now, and you can see, feel, and sense all the thoughts melting away from your mind with each breath. You are insulated against outside noises and are now letting go of any worry, stress, or concerns from your day and week.

Take a moment now to focus on your body and allow the relaxing waves of the divine to wash over you starting at the top of your head, flowing down over your head and shoulders, over your torso and waist, down over your hips and thighs, to your calves and feet. Allow the relaxing waves of divine support and healing to continue to repeat moving over your body, removing more of anything unneeded each time those waves roll over you.

Feel those relaxing waves of energy permeating the core of your being and flowing through each organ, cell, and tissue going down to your toes, providing a space of inner deep healing. Feel those waves further deepening your own sense of relaxation now as you release completely into this moment.

For a moment, bring your awareness to your inner vision. Go now to your own inner sanctuary in your mind's eye. In this place you have grown so familiar with, you are able to connect with your spirit guides, animal guides, and loved ones in spirit. It is a sacred, safe space for release and renewal.

Notice yourself walking about your own inner sanctuary now. This time, instead of focusing on what you are seeing, you are now only paying attention to what it is you are hearing. As you take a step, what does it sound like? You may be wondering how on earth you are supposed to hear anything with ear plugs or headphones in; however, notice how enhanced your own inner hearing has become, the quieter your surroundings.

What sound do the leaves on the trees make around you? Or the water of the stream, or the waves of the ocean? Depending on where your own inner sanctuary is, allow its natural sounds to magnify and provide a soundscape of multiple sounds happening at once. Do you hear any animal sounds? Anything flying overhead? Do you hear the ringing of a bell in the distance, or the sounds of moving objects nearby? Can you hear the distant sound of children's laughter? Or in your personal sanctuary is there silence?

Hear now the sound of a being of light walking toward you. It sounds louder and louder as they approach you now. You may be experiencing multiple sensations at once. Avoid scattering your focus by trying to see or feel anything at all. Pull all of your focus into what it is you are hearing only. Does someone say hello? What is the sound of their voice like? Can you make out if it is a high or low voice? A sharp or a soft voice? Pay attention to the tone and timber of their vocal sounds. How does it make you feel to have them near you, making a connection?

Allow yourself to greet them now. Ask them who they are or what they are doing here. Offer the chance for them to reply. It should come with ease; you should not have to wait a long period of time to hear them. Should you find yourself struggling, invite them to come closer to you, and inform them you intend to listen to what insights they have for you right now at this point in your life.

Now it's time to begin writing. You are allowed to open your eyes, glance down at a blank page in your notebook, and just start writing what you hear. At first it may come in short phrases or short sentences. That is perfectly fine.

Next, write down a question for spirit to come through with an answer. Good questions for this portion of the meditation are: "What do I need to know right now?" or something even more specific such as "What is the true purpose of life?" or "What can be of most benefit to humanity right now?" You will now write for a full ten minutes without stopping. It will seem like an eternity, but I must stress—do not stop writing. Your words and sentences may run together. Don't edit, don't go back and re-read, just write. It may not even make sense to you in your head.

At some point, you will feel a switch turn on. Something will shift and it will flow as if the pen is leading you, rather than you leading the pen or waiting for words. When ten minutes has ended, put your pen down. Take a nice deep breath; release anything not needed down your grounding cords.

Read what you wrote from beginning to end. Follow the tips for best use.

Helpful Guidance: Don't judge this process. In the beginning it feels really strange, but if you stick with it and look back over your notes, you will be able to see where your own voice stopped and another started. I call those highlighted moments.

monly, claircognizance is experienced as knowing something without really knowing *how*.

Some believe the received information and certainty are transferred to us by divine beings such as angels, spirit guides, or connection with other supportive forces of the universe. I most definitely believe the gift of claircognizance comes from within yourself. People with this gift have a built-in antenna that is always up and ready for when the information or insight is needed. No matter where it comes from or how it works, the access point is through the crown chakra, or the body's wisdom center, located at the top of the head.

Claircognizants are typically who people rely on in times of pressure or in fast-paced work environments for answers. It's as if people with this gift have a huge database in their minds—with very little effort, answers and ideas come to them spontaneously, as if out of the blue. They are also the ones with the deepest inner hunches when something is on or off, though they may not be able to say why. The encouragement to grow your gift of claircognizance is to increase the speed at which you attain insights for yourself or others. It can be confusing for some people to know things without knowing how, but it's a great exercise in surrendering to your higher self.

TOOLS

Two great tools for working with claircognizance are using a pendulum, and scrying, also known as crystal ball gazing. When you focus and concentrate on something, the inner knowing can grow even stronger. While gazing at a crystal, have someone ask you a question for guidance or clarity and see what you get! Exercises such as scrying break up the monotony of sitting in silence, waiting for something to come to you. With a pendulum, try to guess the answers before the pendulum gives them to you and then see if you are right.

The Akashic Records are another entryway to metaphysical knowledge that can be accessed from the physical plane. The Akashic Records are a record house that exists in the non-physical etheric plane of existence which holds every bit of information from the entire human experience that has ever gone before and will ever be. They contain the history of the universe, including each soul's karmic history. People gifted with claircognizance have easier access to this place, and spiritual information and knowledge can directly come through the crown chakra into a sense of knowing.

The following meditation will grant you access to the Akashic Records. The first thing to do is ponder a question or area of life, humanity, or the world you would like to explore and know more about. Write it down in your journal. Keep your journal and pen handy, for whatever you might experience through exploring the Records.

Please allow a full twenty minutes to complete this meditation from beginning to end. If you have more time to set aside for journaling, it would offer you plenty of unrushed time to feel into it.

MEDITATION

Find yourself in a comfortable position. This meditation may be done either seated or lying down. I find it much more comfortable to lie down for this particular one, as it brings you to such a dreamy space, and it can feel so good to have your whole body supported. It is also important with this meditation not to have any outside disturbances, distractions, or noise interferences. You may find soft background music helpful to enhancing and deepening the relaxation portion of this meditation.

At the beginning of this meditation, you will be spending time going into a deeply relaxed state. The more time you spend in the relaxation, the easier it will be to bring in information from the Akasha.

Close your eyes and begin with your breath, slowing the pace of your breathing to one that feels more calming and comfortable. Notice the air flowing in and out of your lungs, and for a moment just feel into it. Breathe in and out, in and out; each time you breathe out, say to yourself the word "release" as you allow all the care, tension, concern, or weight of your day to move down your grounding chords and be safely transported away from your body. Repeat this cycle of breathing at least ten full rotations before moving on.

Tell yourself with each breath out that you are growing exponentially more relaxed. Feel all the muscles, tissues, organs, and membranes of your body fully release and relax. With each breath out, allow yourself to go even more deeply into this wonderful flow of calm. Continue breathing for some time. Take your time. This is the relaxation portion of this meditation. It shouldn't be rushed.

With each breath, you feel your thoughts beginning to slow down. You find now as you take even another breath, you are having a more difficult time holding your thought processes as concrete thought begins to dissolve. You can feel your thoughts gradually disintegrating and leaving your mind. When you are finished with this meditation, you can come back to them, fully restored.

As you adjust and shift your body to become even more comfortable, you allow your breath to deepen your state of relaxation even further, and you find your body beginning now to sink into the object you are lying or sitting on. It feels as if the entire room and building fully supports your own release. You have nothing to worry about and nowhere to be right now. This is a time for you to just let it all go; there's no need to hold it together—you can just set your life aside like a big, heavy trunk to wait while you take this exciting journey of discovery.

You find yourself now on a grassy hillside, wandering toward a destination. As you walk, in the distance you hear running water, like a stream or river flowing nearby. You walk toward the sound, and find a canoe docked on the shore. You are compelled to get in, and lie down in the soft blankets that are covering the bottom. You pull the oars inside and lie back, somehow knowing that the boat will float to its intended destination. All you need do is relax and look up at the sky, watch the clouds float by overhead, and feel yourself being gently rocked back and forth, back and forth.

As the canoe moves further and further away from the shore, you become aware of the lulling sensation of the water and the warm sun on your body. Each gentle sway of the canoe takes you even deeper, more and more relaxed. You feel so at ease with this journey, knowing now you are getting closer and closer to your destination.

After some time, the canoe gently stops. You notice someone standing before you: a guide to help you out of the canoe and onto dry land. You understand and know instantly that you are in safe hands, and follow this guide to a large set of stairs leading upward to a large wooden door.

With each step you go up, you feel something shifting inside; your body now responds with gentle tingling, numbness, and pressure. You know you are getting close to exploring the Akashic Records. The guide continues to lead you up the stairs, and you know you are getting closer to the top. The guide takes out a key and opens the large wooden door, granting you entry.

You walk into the Akashic Records and are greeted by what appears to be largest record-keeping place you have ever seen. You see, feel, know that there are methods for keeping record in endless amounts. It is mystifying and baffling to you how there could be so much stored here.

You wander for a while and then you find yourself standing before one kind of record-keeping area. This is the area where you will discover information in the form of knowing for the question or area you brought into this meditation. You take a moment and pause before gathering what it is you came for: some nugget of wisdom, a morsel of knowledge, a glimmer of insight. You are patient and take your time, waiting until it feels complete.

You have gathered everything you needed for this time, and this question. The guide appears to lead you back to the wooden door, down the staircase, and to your canoe once more, gently help you in, and you find yourself in awe of what you just experienced. The water gently rocks you back and forth, as you are guided back across the water to the other shore. Once landed, you dock, and come back into your body. Take nice deep breaths, and release anything you no longer wish to keep from your experience; hold only the most important things.

You may open your eyes and journal what you experienced in as much detail as you can recall.

Helpful Guidance: The next time you are trying to figure something out and your logical brain is stumped, whether it's your boss's motivations or the quickest way to get your afternoon errands accomplished, silently ask your intuition to give you the answer through claircognizance. Your intuition is always listening and could have some amazing answers for you.

FOR YOUR JOURNAL

What was it like going on this journey? What did you experience, see, feel, know? Did you feel supported? What was it like being in the Akasha? What sort of record-keeping mechanism did you encounter? What insight did you receive?

SEVEN
The Chakras

A chakra is an invisible wheel or disk of energy that resides in the auric field of every person. The seven main chakras begin at the top of the head, and go down the spine to the tailbone. Knowledge of the chakras has transferred to our Western culture first from Ayurveda, from India. Modern-day healing practitioners use this knowledge in conjunction with many other forms of alternative or energy healing, often as a basis for understanding and detecting what areas of the body and of life need attention, correction, and healing.

The chakras are associated with different areas of life (from top to bottom): wisdom, clarity, communication, love, power, trust, and security. They are also associated with different organs, glands and regions of the body. The knowledge of the chakras provides a basis for understanding regarding how the spiritual and physical bodies engage, merge, and interact. What impacts the chakras often impacts the physical body, and vice versa.

An image that may be familiar to you is a curled-up snake resting at the tailbone, uncoiling and rising up the spine, also known as kundalini awakening. As this snake rises up, it is said to spontaneously initiate various different spiritual and healing processes, ultimately contributing to a profound sense of spiritual transformation. In many spiritual philosophies, our path here is one of continuous expansion of consciousness with the aim of achieving enlightenment. By allowing the snake to rise up, the chakras are activated and opened, and you are supporting your own spiritual growth and expansion.

The philosophies of many Eastern medicine healing modalities are the same: when you tend to afflictions located in the spirit body, the auric field, and the chakras, you directly affect the physical body's natural healing capability. There are situational, psychic, mental, and emotional episodes in our lives that can dramatically affect the chakras. If those episodes are offered time and attention to heal, the chakras can be restored, offering a spiritual armor to further protect those situations from permeating the auric field and thus harming the physical body.

My personal philosophy is one of balance. Tending to both the chakras and the physical body, combining both Eastern and Western medicine models, affords a more holistic approach to ongoing care. Building in a self-care routine through chakra meditation is a way to build that spiritual armor, healing anything that may have impacted your chakra system. Chakra meditation and care is a simple preventative step promoting spiritual, emotional, and physical healing.

Taking care of your chakras not only impacts your physical and spiritual health, it also contributes to the expansion of your psychic abilities. Consider the chakras as a circuitry system. When a circuit is disrupted, it disconnects your natural gifts from functioning at their highest capacity. When one is shut down, it can directly affect the others, setting off a domino effect, until a current once again runs through it. You are the one who can restore them, through meditation, nutrition, breath, yoga stretching, and regular self-care. When the circuitry is working well and smoothly, you are better able to connect to psychic information and messages.

Clairvoyants often visualize the chakras during meditation and often describe them as colorful, circulating orbs. Clairsentients feel the colors surging through their bodies, clairaudients can hear the color names or receive information about which chakras need the most healing, and claircognizants have an inner knowing about which chakras are in need of attention and nurturing.

SEVEN BASIC CHAKRAS

First chakra: Also known as the root chakra, located at the base of your spine at your tailbone. The color associated with this chakra is red. It is associated with security and safety.

Second chakra: Known as the navel or sacral chakra, located in the sacrum region, right behind your belly button. The color is orange. It is associated with trust and intimacy.

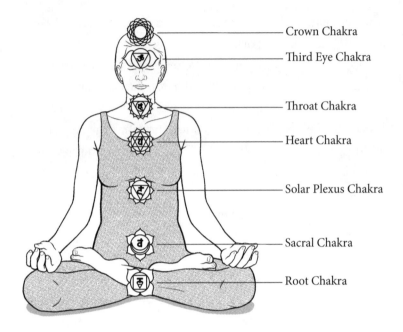

Crown Chakra

Third Eye Chakra

Throat Chakra

Heart Chakra

Solar Plexus Chakra

Sacral Chakra

Root Chakra

Third chakra: Located in your solar plexus below your chest and above your belly. The color is yellow. This is your personal power chakra.

Fourth chakra: Also known as your heart chakra, located in the center of your chest. The color is green. It is associated with unconditional love and compassion.

Fifth chakra: Also known as your throat chakra. The color is blue. This chakra is associated with personal truth, communication, and self-expression.

Sixth chakra: Your third eye chakra, this chakra is located between your eyebrows. The color is purple. This chakra connects to your inner vision.

Seventh chakra: Also known as the crown chakra, located at the top of your head. The color is indigo, white, or gold. This chakra connects you to divine wisdom and knowledge.

There are simple ways to detect which chakra is off-balance and needs your attention the most. Headaches are associated with your sixth or seventh chakras; heartburn or indigestion is associated with the fourth chakra; constipation shows up in the second chakra; bloating is a third chakra affliction, and a recurring sore throat is connected to the fifth chakra. These are just some examples of ways to begin directing your own attention and awareness to understand what is happening in your etheric body. Strengthening the chakras through meditation, essential oils, yoga, healing modalities, and nutrition is a wonderful way to support and promote ongoing healing of the physical and spiritual bodies.

EIGHT
Chakra Meditation

We begin in the root chakra, which helps us with our own most basic and fundamental security needs and is also associated with survival. Excessive focus on basic needs and survival strains this chakra, as well as extended periods of being unable to meet basic needs. Personal feelings of insecurity also negatively affect this chakra, so being able to directly address, deal with, and heal insecurities is one way to help it thrive.

When we move beyond the first chakra to the second chakra of trust and intimacy, we have done the work of securing our place in the world; we know where we belong. We move from the second chakra when we have achieved the ability to trust ourselves and the world and also form intimate bonds with our loved ones. The second chakra may not be as vibrant when desires to make healthy changes are thwarted due to fear of the unknown. Learning to trust the self and the goodness in others, along with taking appropriate risks and action steps to forward your own life path, greatly benefit this sensitive chakra. In relationships, increasing physical touch and intimacy can have tremendous supportive and enhancing benefits to the second chakra.

After this, our evolution leads us into the work of the third chakra, the home of our personal power and our own sense of confidence as we stand upright in the world, ready and willing to assert our self and address our needs. When we are unable to feel as if we are living a life of purpose or when we do what others want of us instead of what we need to do for ourselves, this chakra is afflicted. This area is most commonly suffering in people who have been told or believe they aren't good enough. When you hear those messages enough times, you begin to believe it. Working on eliminating those thoughts and adapting a narrative that allows for a greater sense of self adds tremendously to feelings of confidence and causes us to stand upright in the world.

Up to the heart chakra we go. The work here is to develop a path rooted deeply in empathy and compassion both for self and others. The act of forgiveness also heals the heart chakra, as it can release energetic links to those who have harmed you. The heart chakra is challenged when resentments and anger toward others are held there for long durations. Feelings of hurt and betrayal affect this chakra deeply, and empaths in particular will feel the effects most strongly, as much of the processing of the world filters through the heart. Keeping the heart open and supple is an ongoing task, and learning to create a boundary between you and the problems and traumas of others can assist in supporting the ongoing opening of your own heart center.

Offering love freely can be challenging for many, but over time, it strengthens this important chakra, the generator of the spiritual body.

Then we move on to the throat or the fifth chakra. This is where our truth and self-expression lives. When we have mastered the ability to communicate our truth with passion and devotion, we are keeping this chakra open and rotating with ease. In our hesitancy to speak up, or share our own beliefs, ideas, and perspectives, we cause this chakra to seize up. Have you ever felt a knot in your throat or as though you were being choked as you held back what you needed to say? Finding ways to gently yet firmly speak your own truth will keep this chakra open and flowing, offering a greater sense of balance and the ability to assert your perspectives. Expressing too many of your thoughts and opinions can also strain and over-stress your fifth chakra. Learn to temper these moments with levity, knowing you cannot (nor should) fight every battle.

Next we move along to our third eye, or the sixth chakra, the bottomless well of deep clarity and understanding. The chapter on activating your third eye is a wonderful supplement to keeping your third eye activated and happy. Keeping this chakra vibrant is rooted in allowing your own inner vision to support your life choices. Noticing and paying attention to your inner vision; and using the images, symbols, and pictures to support your life path keeps this chakra vibrant. When we choose skepticism over openness, our third eye becomes sluggish and our vision becomes clouded. One way to keep this chakra vibrant is to keep a journal. When you have visions, see things that cause you to pause, or have spiritual experiences you wonder about, writing them down can help add validity over time to the supportive visions you were given.

Finally, with the rising up of the energetic snake from our root chakra all the way up to the seventh chakra, we have burst our consciousness open to a magnificent state of connection with the divine. Imagine a beautiful white funnel open at the top, extending itself to the cosmos or the divine. When the seventh chakra is closed, our sense of oneness with all things and spiritual connectedness is cut off. In that space, feelings of isolation and loneliness become the norm. Our ability to connect with the wisdom in the universe is available and channels down through our crown, or seventh chakra. As in all things, there are multiple ways to achieve this divine and cosmic connection; meditation is but one way.

In her book *Wheels of Life: A User's Guide to the Chakra System*, author and chakra expert Anodea Judith reveals a powerful philosophy about the reasons for connecting with and fostering a nurturing relationship with the chakras:

> I firmly believe that clearing the chakras through understanding their nature, practicing related exercises, and using visualization and meditation, prepares the way for a spiritual opening that is apt to be less tumultuous than is so often the case for Kundalini awakenings. I believe this Westernization is an important step for speaking to the Western mind in a way that is har-

monious with the circumstances in which we
live, rather than antithetical to it. It gives us a
context in which these experiences can occur.

The goal of this chakra meditation is to assist you in releasing
any residual invisible yet powerful energetic blockages around
and through your chakra system for the purpose of achieving
a heightened sense of awareness, expanded consciousness, and
spiritual strength. While there are hundreds of chakras throughout the physical and etheric bodies, we are going to focus on the
seven primary chakras. This will provide you the beginning of a
long and beautiful healing journey.

The following meditation is different from the others; it
is important to go in order. In addition, please do not let this
meditation's simplicity lead you to think it is less powerful than
the others. To the contrary, it is equally if not more powerful
because it serves a three-pronged purpose: bringing awareness of any challenged chakras, removing any blockages, and
strengthening the energy field to build resistance against dis-
ease. In the process of healing and strengthening, the psychic
receiving centers in your body more readily receive insights and
information. This meditation should take ten to fifteen minutes.
As with all meditations, it may take longer the first few times
until you get the hang of it.

MEDITATION

Close your eyes and connect with your breath. Become aware
of your own etheric field, the invisible energy field around your

body. Notice for a moment how far out into space it extends from your own body. Practice now expanding and contracting your own etheric body (also known as an aura). Notice what it feels like to expand your etheric body outward into space all around you, filling up the room you are in. Now bring it back, contracting it until it is like a thin skin lining your physical body. Notice how it feels. Settle in to the awareness that you are more than a physical body. Notice any colors or sensations.

Breathe and release yourself in the relaxation provided by this moment. Shift your focus and attention to the base of your spine, right at your tailbone. Notice a red orb of light hovering around the base of your spine, circulating, rotating, and moving in through your body, and out again. With your inner awareness, expand that root chakra, moving what is now a horizontal column of red light out the front of your body into space, and again out the back of you. Say to yourself, "I am safe and secure." Remain focused in the root chakra, until you feel the red column of light has removed any barriers to its own openness.

Continue to breathe and release, breathe and release. Anything that shows up as discomfort, you can simply breathe and set it free. Anything that no longer serves you dissipates with your breath.

Now, move your focus to the area in your navel, just around your belly button. See, feel, and sense the orb of light, the color orange hovering there. With your mind, begin moving it in a circular motion: the brightest color orange glowing now, rotating, beginning to move outward from the front of your body into space, out behind your body, that orange column of light clearing and removing any residual or stuck energy. Say to your-self, "I trust myself and others." Remain in this space with your own awareness until you feel that area of your body is clear and open.

Move your attention up to your solar plexus, to the space above your navel, and below your chest. This is the third chakra, and its color is yellow. Breathe deeply now and see, feel, and sense that bright column as yellow as the sun, moving in and out of your body out the front of you into space, and again out the back of you. Feel it releasing any further barriers to your own sense of self. Say to yourself, "I am powerful beyond measure."

Breathe and open, breathe and open, moving up to the heart chakra, located in the center of your chest, represented by the color green. Focus on moving that beautiful emerald column of light out the front of your body, into the room you are in and beyond, again out your back, between your shoulders. Feel yourself relax into the good feelings of breathing into this open-hearted space, where even more clarity and understanding is available to you. Say to yourself, "I am love."

Move your attention up to your throat chakra, the color blue. Pause for a moment and notice the brilliance of the hue. With a simple thought, you are able to move this horizontal column of light out into space in front of you and out the back of your neck. If you feel discomfort or a welling up of emotion, sim-ply allow that emotion to flow. You are being cleansed by your own emotion, able now to release what it is that has been held trapped inside of you, just by sinking into the full expression of who you are. Say to yourself, "I express the truth of who I am."

Move up now to your forehead or third eye chakra. See, sense, or feel an orb whose color is purple. Expand that orb outward into space, in front of you and behind you. Feel yourself letting down the barriers and walls built up around you, connecting to and restoring your own inner sense of clarity. Notice any changes in the way your body feels, such as tingling, numbness, or pressure. Say to yourself, "I release myself into full awareness."

At the top of your head, now in the seventh chakra, move the indigo, white, or gold orb of light outward into space in front of you, and again behind. You are aware of a horizontal column of light that expands and contracts at will. This is the location of your own internal wise being. This is where you have access to greater knowledge and understanding; where you make connections to the wisdom of your life experiences, and lives before this one. Say to yourself, "I am one with the divine."

Continue to breathe and release any further discomfort or unwanted energy you may have picked up during this meditation. When your body and aura shifts to find a greater harmony, at times there may be occasional discomfort. This is nothing to worry about. Just keep moving the discomfort with your breath.

Helpful Guidance: I recommend music with this meditation, something fluid and beautiful, instrumental, without words. It may greatly deepen the results.

FOR YOUR JOURNAL

How do you experience your chakras during the meditation? Do you see, feel, sense, or just know they are moving? What other things did you see, sense, or feel during this meditation?

NINE

Activate Your Third Eye Meditation

The third eye is a natural part of every person. The third eye is a very clever bit of everyone's innate abilities that allows you to see, sense, and detect the patterns in your life, in coordination with the universe. It operates like the lens of a film projector, and acts as the window between the spiritual realms and the screen, represented by all of your other senses.

Your third eye can be used in many different ways. Seers use their third eye to understand hidden connections and answer questions. Energy workers "feel" the energies around them and can then consciously manipulate that energy. And every time you have empathy, you are using your third eye to touch and feel the emotions of others. In hindsight, my own third eye was opening during my childhood. I had many spiritual experiences of "seeing" and sensing spirits wandering around my home, especially at night. When I reflect back to my youth, I have strong memories surfacing where I knew and felt things others around me didn't. At the time, I knew I was different. I kept much of that to myself out of fear of judgment.

A common misperception is that activating the third eye will help you see things in your future playing out, like on a movie screen. This is not its purpose nor how it works. The reason for working on activating the third eye is for the rest of your psychic gifts to become amplified. It's the charger to your already existing gifts, whether clairvoyant (clear seeing), clairsentient (clear feeling), clairaudient (clear hearing), or clair-cognizant (clear knowing). The third eye is the gateway to all other realms and the collective or universal mind. Imagine all of your senses, including your sixth sense, harmonized and open. Once the third eye activates, what's possible includes access to other realms and spiritual dimensions. It is also worth noting that fully opening your third eye could take years, if not the rest of your life, which is why I prefer the term "activate" rather than "opening." It's not the goal to expect your third eye to be completely open. The goal is to strive for mini-activations taken in baby steps or bite-sized chunks on a regular basis.

What you do not need to do is go to a chakra-opening guru or practitioner who claims to be able to open your third eye. Be wary of anyone claiming they can do this for you. Your third eye will activate naturally and gradually on its own, and in its own good time. A commonly held belief is the idea that by opening your third eye, you will dramatically change your life and no longer experience negativity or struggle. The truth is that no one is insulated from the human condition; it affects us all.

Briefly, some of the common warning signs your third eye chakra is afflicted are: insomnia; confusion, anxiety, or difficulty in making decisions; being creatively blocked; poor memory; frequent headaches; a consistent feeling of uncertainty about what to do with your life; a strong pull to meditate, be in silence, and do restorative activities. I typically feel a dull melancholy wash over me and an inability to focus. In those moments, all I want to do is lie down and sleep. When I focus on lifting the blocks, something is restored inside as things suddenly begin to "click" better. Well, that, and a good long nap usually does the trick as well!

During the process of activating your third eye, you may encounter some unusual experiences, some of the most common of which are covered here. As with all things related to psychic development, many of the experiences you will have are pleasant. However, some will confuse you or even make you feel fearful if you don't expect them. You may note in the margins what things you have actually already experienced, as it was likely the activation of your third eye but you didn't even realize it.

Your dreams may become more vivid and you can remember them better. You feel more peaceful. Some people reporting the ability to feel and see invisible beings. You may experience déjà vu more often. You are likely to notice symbols, clues, and signs in your external environment that validate your own personal experiences. You may hear things other people don't. You may have visions or see things others don't. You feel the need to meditate more. You become more creative and full of creative ideas. You may know something before it happens. You may become more clear about your purpose in this life. You meet your spirit guide or feel as though you're being guided. You feel other people's emotions. You see auras. You often have a gut feeling (intuition). You have a tingling feeling near your third eye chakra. You (sometimes) see energy flowing and moving through the room in the form of light clouds, white or purple sparkles, or flashes dashing about.

You can be assured that your third eye is activating if you close your eyes and can see patterns of color behind your eyelids: white/blue/purple swirls of colors, intense white dots, black sky with numerous stars, or the shape of the eye/square/circle/some other shape filled with blue or purple color. These are all positive signs that you have activated your third eye. You may not have all of these experiences, and that doesn't mean your third eye isn't responding; it's just different for everyone. If you feel the pressure or some activity in the middle of your forehead, that means that your third eye is being activated and soon you may be able to see color and other phenomena. Some of your visions will not make any sense to you, and others will be so vivid that you'd swear they were actually happening right in front of you. There are all kinds of dimensions out there, and with your third eye activated you will be able to pick up on them. The higher vibration you offer, the higher developed worlds you will be able to explore.

TOOLS

In moments where your third eye is too open, you are more susceptible to experiencing a flood of overwhelming phenomena, similar to empathy fatigue (see chapter 4). When I was first awakening my own psychic gifts, my third eye was quite active. I recall having an endless stream of psychic experiences that, although exciting, was simply too much at times. To calm down my third eye, I would use my grounding meditation to focus the energies and release them to the earth. You can use this simple tool as well. Remember that your third eye is connected to your sixth chakra. You can gently close your sixth chakra and hence positively affect your third eye by visualizing a beautiful indigo-colored flower gently closing its petals around your forehead. Visualization and intention in general are effective ways of disconnecting from moments that are overwhelming or negative. You may also wish to take off your shoes and ground to the earth's energy. Grounding brings you right back into your body and gently stops the flow of energy around that part of your sensory system. After a long day of doing readings at a psychic fair, I typically enjoy a nice big meal of warm, comforting foods. These are all simple and effective ways to tend to and manage your own personal energy.

For the following meditation, please allocate a full twenty minutes. Unlike the other meditations in this book, this one can take the most time, as it requires you to adjust to slowing down the mind and body to get fully into the groove. You will tend to the relaxation of the physical body and mind more than anything else. For some it could take up to thirty minutes. Please allow yourself this beautiful space and come back to this meditation often; it is one of the cornerstones of building your psychic abilities.

You can sit in a chair or lie down on a bed, but I have found sitting on the floor on a cushion to be the most beneficial. For the most benefit, sit in the lotus position to ensure your chakras are aligned. I like to imagine someone or something above me is gently pulling the grounding string of light going up through my spine and out the top of my head.

MEDITATION

Begin by relaxing each muscle in your body, starting with your toes and working all the way up to the top of your head. Draw your attention to your feet. Actively tense and then release them. Move up to your calves. Tense the muscles and release with your breath, up to your thighs, and so on until you reach your face and the top of your head. Tend to your breath, slowing it down ever so slightly. Take your time and begin again if you still feel tension anywhere in your body. Visualize or feel each muscle, bone, and ligament responding to your requests for relaxation.

Breathe in for a count of five, and exhale for a count of five until all the air has expelled from your lungs. Repeat this again several times. Feel your mind and body relaxing. Watch your breath and become one with this life force. Your mind comes to center. Notice how much deeper your meditation experience goes. Be with this breath rotation until your body is loose. Your mind is now calm and relaxed.

See, sense, and feel the waves of calm energy come over your body. Feel its warmth permeate your being as it rises up through your body. Rest in this space for several moments before moving on. Slowly draw the energy to the center of your head, in between your eyebrows. Notice the sensations: tingling, pressure, and numbness are all completely normal responses to this.

Don't try to stop thinking; just let go of attachments and aversions as if nothing matters. Feel yourself becoming lighter and lighter, as you feel gravity now falling away.

Bring your attention back to your breath. Stay with it and visualize an indigo ball of light turning in a complete rotation at the center of your mind. This ball of light is vibrantly pulsing. It is sparkling, growing with momentum. Be with this for several moments.

See and feel this ball expanding and fully accept its presence. As it expands, the indigo color streams out through the center of your forehead. Continue to let go of thoughts; let them arrive and depart as they occur.

Now let the indigo light in even more. Remain open to seeing whatever is put before you—pictures, colors, information, or nothing.

This is an appropriate time to call upon your spirit guide, angel, or master to assist with the process. Feel yourself surrendering in complete trust for your guide's interest in your well-being and safety.

The experience may naturally move you into a dreamy state as it becomes much more difficult to hold your thoughts. Instead, you feel yourself surrendering to the bliss of an even flow. You release yourself now on the waves of energy surrounding you. Feel it lift you up and out of this physical experience. Sense your connection to the power of the universe, to all that is.

You feel as though you are being lifted up and out of yourself, your human form now moving further away as you are free to explore. Lift higher, and with a thought you are there with the stars, able to travel to other realms, other worlds, wherever your third eye wishes to take you. You are no longer limited by this earthly experience and you surrender now to the grand adventure. Take as much time as you wish to explore.

Gently invite yourself to come back, and feel yourself being pulled back down slowly into the room where your body lies. You return once more to your body, safe and sound. Breathe and release the breath down your grounding cords. Tether yourself here until the next adventure.

Helpful Guidance: Be patient with your progress. Activating your third eye is different from opening your third eye. Enjoy the sensations no matter how subtle. Journal and keep track of any shifts you feel, know, or see every time you do this one.

FOR YOUR JOURNAL

What experiences, visions, or sensations did you have during the third eye activation meditation?

TEN

Enhancing Intuition Meditation

Your intuition feeds your psychic abilities. In addition, intuition and psychic gifts are often mistaken for one another. While they operate and function in similar ways, the processes for information gathering are completely different. What strengthens your intuition strengthens your psychic abilities, making it a worthwhile part of any psychic development practice.

Intuition is the internal compass within us all. It's our gut or where we get the hunch that something isn't quite right. Intuition is the already built-in operating system of our internal knowing. It guides our actions and footsteps without necessarily knowing the outcome. Our psychic gifts can solidify information of the unknown about the past, present, or possible future. People who use both psychic and intuitive abilities in a professional capacity are known as psychic intuitives. Let's first break down the differences and then discuss how naturally intuition and psychic abilities work together in harmony.

Let's say you are at a party with someone but you hardly know anyone else present. Your friend introduces you to someone and while shaking their hand, a bad feeling washes over you. You get a vibe from this person that you do not like, though you don't quite know why. That information causes you to distance yourself from that person for the rest of the evening. By the end of the night you overhear them backstabbing the friend you came with. Your intuitive hunch was accurate to avoid speaking with them. This is your innate intuition in action.

Now let's say at that same party, you meet someone new and while speaking with them, you suddenly see an image in your mind of a beautiful boat, and that person you are chatting with is standing on the boat waving at you to come aboard and join them. It is an interesting image that you take note of to analyze later. You exchange contact information. They call you the following week to ask you about a business opportunity. In that moment, the vision of the boat pops into your mind. The business opportunity, if you take it, will require some travel overseas. This is an example of your psychic abilities in action. An image, symbol, or metaphor appears to clarify a situation or event from the past, present, or future.

We use our intuition for moment-to-moment decision making. Our environment provides our intuition with the clues, cues, and validation we need to make the best decisions. When you work on developing your intuition, you actively send out your sixth sense antennae while adjusting your own frequency to align with your surroundings. The signals and signs your antennae pick up from your environment are a result of refining your intuitive muscle. For example, after a meditation you take a walk in the woods. While you are walking, you see a cardinal cross your path. Your intuition has drawn to this nature messenger quite naturally, though seemingly by coincidence. Our intuition collaborates with our surroundings when our vibrational frequency is strongest. Keeping your intuition strong allows your psychic abilities to develop much more easily.

Over time and with diligent attention, your intuition and your environment link up to continue to provide what you need. Some highly intuitive people often comment that they feel at one with their surroundings, as they take the information provided by their sixth sense quite seriously. Over time, they have learned to trust the input. To more greatly understand what's being given to you, an intuition journal is highly recommended.

Remember that using your intuition isn't only confined to hunches and gut feelings of something being off. It is in collaboration with your surroundings and with the support of psychic tools that you become an information gatherer, of sorts.

Here's what using your intuition can do for you:

1. Diminishes stress by assisting you in solving current life problems.
2. Boosts imagination and creativity.
3. Makes your life feel on track.
4. Improves your relationships when you can better sense and tune in to the needs of others.
5. Can help you clarify your true purpose in life.
6. Can help you narrowly avoid catastrophe when followed.

7. Makes you more sensitive to your environment and the people around you.

8. Strengthens your psychic gifts.

Ways to develop your intuition:

1. Pay attention to your dreams. They are your own concerns and fears, secret desires, playing out during your sleep. Keep a dream journal by your bed, to record when you wake.

2. Meditate.

3. Develop creative hobbies.

4. Spend time in nature.

5. Notice your body's reactions to the events and circumstances in your life.

6. Journal life events and pay particular attention to hindsight to assist in course correction.

7. Go with your hunches rather than fighting them. In time, you'll grow to trust them more.

8. Envision a conversation with a wise master, where you ask questions and are given answers.

9. Anticipate and track outcomes for future review.

10. Flip a coin when making an important decision. Before you do anything, check in and imagine what taking that action feels like. That is your intuition giving you information.

The following meditation takes fifteen to twenty minutes. I would recommend playing calm music in the background, if you find it helps you relax easily. As this meditation's main purpose is to relax the mind and release the thoughts, a sitting position is best so as not to fall asleep.

MEDITATION

Begin by finding a comfortable position and closing your eyes. Your attention now begins to travel inward. You may be noticing any tension or energy you wish to release from your day and allow this to leave you, surrendering fully into the moment.

Become present to your breath. Allow the stream of air coming into your lungs and out your mouth to find a smooth, easy pace. For the time being, all you need to do is focus on your breath. With each breath you take, notice yourself resting more easily in the chair you are sitting in. It feels so good to take these few moments to dedicate to your own relaxation.

Intuition comes from the steady place within that is beyond thought or emotion, and now is the time to access that place. You may be aware of thoughts and feelings. Simply be aware of whatever it is you are experiencing in the moment. Allow yourself to become fully present; take in the sounds and scents, and simply notice and let go of any feelings about it. What is going on within you? Are any thoughts coming and going? You don't need to try pushing anything aside. Instead, follow whatever appears until it becomes a meaningless activity.

Continue now to be easily aware of what is happening. You are not resisting anything, trying to change anything, or making anything happen. Now bring your awareness to your breath again. Notice your breath moving in and out of your body. Your life and surroundings assist in contributing to your own inner knowing. Allow the breath to flow through you; release that which no longer serves you.

Naturally notice sensations in the body now. Let them be like waves of the ocean, letting your awareness sink deeper into the silent depths within, with each breath going deeper and deeper within. All the thinking and noises take place in the background of your own silence within. Allow the mind to drop into that stillness with each breath in and out, in and out. Go to this steady place within.

Allow all the activity of thinking and feeling to happen on the surface. With each passing moment your attention goes more to that steady, still place within. Allow your awareness to sink within even deeper now, with each breath in and out. Allow the awareness to sit in that space of stillness, letting go of everything that is happening around you, including your own thoughts and feelings. Each breath makes it easier to disconnect.

Any time you notice your mind is wandering, don't worry about it. Just breathe and allow yourself to sink deeper within. Let those thoughts be there. Don't judge, and don't analyze what's happening. Let the steady awareness pull you further inside. Intuition is beyond analysis. It's beyond thought. It's beyond emotion. Allow yourself to land on your inner being, the core essence of who you are now.

In this steady place, you can ask a question or bring a situation to mind in need of a solution or answer. Allow the question to appear spontaneously—don't overanalyze the thought or concern. Let the question drop into your own inner knowing and see what answers or feelings arise. Sit for a while with whatever appears; notice any additional insights or feelings. Let go of the need to evaluate the question or concern. If you find yourself becoming emotional about the answer, feeling, or insight, allow the reaction and engage in its release. It's there for a reason.

Answers may come to you as an inner knowing or feeling. Allow yourself now to rest in the strong understanding of the feelings not colored by logic, but instead by feeling. The true answer comes as a certainty or calmness, a certainty or knowing. Trust that calm space of clarity. It feels less like a lightning bolt and more like a warm wash of understanding that flows over you.

Stay in this space for as long as you wish. There is no rush. Take your time, come out slowly, allow yourself to rest in the ease of certainty. When you are ready to move on, open your eyes and journal your experiences, still feeling the expansiveness of your own clarity growing.

Helpful Guidance: declutter a room for this meditation. Having few objects around you clears the energy of a space. This can drive the insights and feelings much deeper.

FOR YOUR JOURNAL

Was this meditation initially easy or difficult for you? Were you able to feel the calm sense of certainty with the answers or confirmation you received regarding your question? Was it easy for you to calm your thoughts by the end, or was it difficult? What information or insights and feelings did you receive regarding your question?

ELEVEN

Grounding for Protection Meditation

Grounding is a concept that refers to being fully present in your own body, and/or being connected to the earth. Grounding exercises clear your mind, calm your emotions, recharge your energy, and strengthen your psychic abilities. I believe our body's natural impulse is to seek out a grounded state. This chapter is about ways in which that can be achieved both for the benefit of the physical body and the opening of your own psychic abilities.

Grounding techniques exist to redistribute energy from your mind to your body. The benefits of regular grounding are: improved blood flow, reduced anxiety, elevated mood, enhanced sleep, and increased memory. Most of the stress we experience is due to a high concentration of energy in our minds, i.e., over-analyzing. The feeling of being unable to shut down the mind is a powerful clue that it's time to get into our grounding routines.

There are many ways to ground your body. One of my favorite ways is through earthing, which is to touch the earth with your bare skin. To put it briefly, when your bare feet or skin comes in contact with the earth, free electrons are taken up into the body. Earth is a conductor for free electrons, as are all living things on the planet, including us. The body is composed of mostly water and minerals, which in combination are excellent conductors of electrons from the earth, provided there is direct skin contact or some other conductive channel for them to flow through. The earth's energy upgrades our own physiology by allowing the body to repair, thereby promoting well-being, vitality, and healthier sleep patterns. It also harmonizes and stabilizes the body's basic biological rhythms. Take a barefooted walk in the grass outside, and for a brief moment notice how your body and mind begin to feel. A charge of energy from the earth begins to harmonize with our own etheric field, bringing about a neutral and balanced flow.

What happens when you aren't grounded:

- You experience excessive worry and anxiety.
- You overanalyze situations and scenarios.
- You feel extremely spaced-out and scattered.
- You get distracted more easily.
- It's easier to suffer from insomnia.
- Your body can be overcome with inflammation.
- Even on days after a good night's sleep, you wake feeling drained and fatigued.
- You are often forgetful or misplace things.

In addition to helping us feel as if we can function better in our daily lives, grounding is a critical component in building our psychic gifts.

When we ground, we calm the over-thinking mind and bring our attention back fully to the present. This enhances the opening of all of our senses, including the sixth sense. In addition, when you begin the process of developing your own psychic abilities, you give permission for your mind and intuition to access information, emotions, symbols, and messages on the inner and outer planes of existence. As a clairvoyant, your visions are heightened and flow more easily. As a clairsentient, you feel things much more deeply. Your inner knowing as a claircognizant intensifies. Grounding is a signal that gives your psychic abilities permission to fly without limits.

Your mind, body, and sixth sense begin dancing together, and that dance is different each time you connect them in meditation. It is exhilarating when that dance begins and the choreography is in harmony. That is when powerful insights are achieved. When my clients in psychic development forget to ground, they often get headaches or feel dizzy or light-headed. They struggle to get the information they crave and begin to doubt their own abilities.

Meditation for psychic development without grounding is like cooking without a pot. What you consume goes everywhere instead of being directed into one particular dish. Grounding is the tethering of your energy to the natural energy field of the earth.

Imagine your own aura, the energy field around you acting much like a sponge. When you open to receive from inner and outer realms of existence, you are also potentially opening up to vibrational frequencies in your environment and from the people you are doing readings with. When our most natural rhythms are thrown off, we struggle to find our own inner sense of balance. Simple things such as thoughts and emotions can leave an energetic imprint on our surroundings and attach themselves to our invisible energy fields. Over time the culmination of those attachments affect our sense of well-being, making it more difficult to freely engage with this beautiful dance of mind and soul, much like covering ourselves with a heavy blanket. You are choosing this meditation as a long-term strategy for keeping your own energy field free and clear of unnecessary extras and as the strongest foundational component of your psychic meditation practice.

Other simple techniques for grounding:

- Hover one hand over your head (crown chakra) for one minute while breathing.
- Close your eyes and put your focus and attention on your feet for two full minutes.
- Observe your breath and clear your mind for five minutes.
- Take a cold shower.
- Wash a sink full of dishes.
- Plant an outdoor or indoor herb garden.
- Take a nap.
- Hug a tree for at least two minutes.

- Try beginning yoga. You can find introductory videos on YouTube for free.
- Declutter a closet and donate items to charity.
- Vacuum for at least ten minutes.
- Wear stone or crystal jewelry that you feel drawn to.
- Carry stones in your pocket.

When you cannot be outside or in colder winter months, the following meditation will produce a similar result to earthing.

MEDITATION

Sit comfortably on a chair or couch, feet on the floor. This meditation shouldn't take more than ten to fifteen minutes.

Relax by closing your eyes and breathing at a slower, more controlled pace. Allow the thoughts from your day or your week to dissipate, each breath relaxing you into a space of neutrality and deep calm.

With each out-breath, say to yourself the word "release." With the power of intention you release whatever no longer serves you: thoughts, emotional energy, fears, physical aches and pains. On the out-breath say to yourself, "I now release what no longer serves me and my highest good."

Imagine next that you have a golden cord of light attached to each of the bottoms of your feet. Those golden cords stretch down all the way to the center of the earth. Feel, sense, or see the chords in your mind's eye as they travel further down, disappearing from sight.

Feel Earth's energy rushing back up the cords to the bottoms of your feet. The energies you released are now restored. Notice how a bright pool of light forms underneath the soles of your feet. Permit the energy to come up through the layers of the earth; up through your feet, into your body, going to each cell, tissue, limb, and organ.

Feel the renewal, cleansing, and healing energy permeate your entire body. Repeat your breathing cycle. Continue to release on your out-breath whatever you no longer want or need. Continue on for several minutes with this rotation of breathing and releasing. Bring white cleansing and healing light up through your body from the earth's core for as long as you wish.

Now imagine those golden cords of light attached at your feet stretching up and merging as one cord of light at the base of your spine, at your tailbone. The golden cord stretches up now through your spine, moving out the top of your head at your crown chakra, extending up into space, connecting you with the divine. You are now an open channel for healing, insight, guidance, and presence.

Center your mind now and calm the dull hum of thoughts you brought with you from your day. Pull your focus from the healing light to a center point in your mind. Find the place right between your eyebrows that represents your third eye. Now travel back a bit further from that point into your mind, and imagine that you are standing in the white room of your mind. There is nothing else in this room with you. You look around and notice an entrance door on one side of the room and an exit door on the other, directly opposite.

Now imagine your thoughts are entering the room and exiting at their own will. Notice the frequency of the activity coming in and going out of the room. Pay attention to the characteristics or qualities of the thoughts entering and exiting the room. Do some linger longer than others?

Approach several of the thoughts now as they come into the room. Introduce yourself to your thoughts. How do they respond to you? Are they kind and welcoming or abrupt and rude? Get to know the personalities of the stream of thoughts going through the room of your mind. Be aware of how it feels to get acquainted with your thinking mind.

Invite all the thoughts to exit the room completely. Now close both the entrance and the exit doors. You are now completely alone in the white room of your mind. There are no more thoughts moving into the room or out of it.

Feel the good feelings of being in this room where there is absolutely nothing tugging at you for your attention. Crack open the entrance door and only let the most cooperative, helpful thoughts in, dismissing the rest.

Now open your heart. Imagine ocean waves of light coming into you from behind, moving out the front of your body into space. Repeat this several times, breathing and releasing any discomfort in your mind or body. Any residual tightness or constriction in your chest is instantly alleviated, as you feel a deeper sense of peace and calm. Feel the good sense surfacing that all is well.

You're relaxing more now into the present moment. Your love and compassion stretch out into the world wherever they need to go. Follow the waves with your inner vision as far as you are able. Continue to allow the waves to stretch out even farther. Notice how wonderful it feels to move into this moment with an open heart.

It's time now to surround yourself with protection. Imagine a large bubble of light surrounding your entire body and etheric field. That bubble may be white, pink, blue, gold, or some other color that calls to you. Feel into the safety of this moment. You are ready to move into the other meditations for psychic development.

Helpful Guidance: Try sitting on the ground outside with bare hands or feet touching the earth.

Always put both feet on the floor to establish optimal conditions for a more solid grounded connection. Have some fun playing with how to get more familiar with your thoughts in the white room of your mind. You may use this meditation at any time, whether or not you are intending to expand yourself psychically. It will definitely provide a sense of peace and calm. Personally, I use this meditation when what I refer to as the "monkey mind" takes hold, where I can't seem to stop the monkeys from running around all over.

FOR YOUR JOURNAL

Recall how you felt before your meditation. Write it down. Observe what shifted in your body or emotions after doing the meditation, and write it down. Continue to track patterns in your ungrounded versus grounded state.

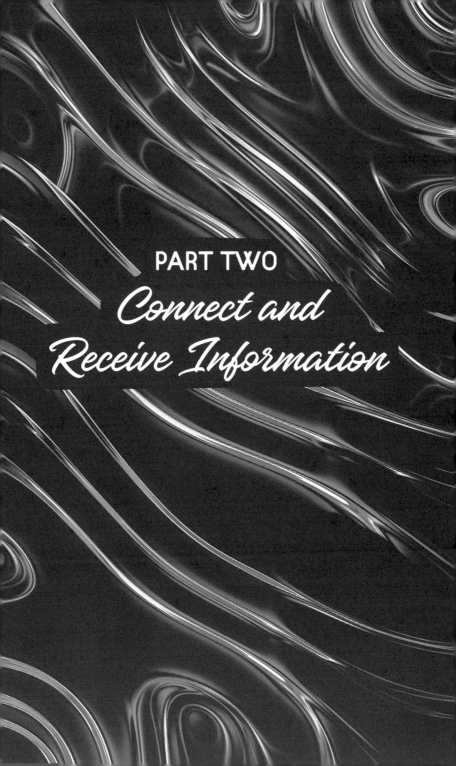

PART TWO

Connect and
Receive Information

TWELVE
Higher Self Meditation

The higher self is an aspect of your higher consciousness. "Higher consciousness" is a term often used by spiritual teachers, and can be a bit challenging to define. So let's consider it in contrast. Much of our lives is spent in lower consciousness, the part of us that tends to our daily survival, tasks, and choices. With greater attention, we can access our higher consciousness, which is simply the spiritual self, not hindered or confined by the physical body or ego.

Consider your higher self the part of you who is always rooting for you, for you to make the best choices, to grow and flourish, the part of you that wants to show you the way forward in life. Another way to think about the higher self is the part of you always connected to Source, that great and everlasting realm of expansiveness, unconditional love, and understanding we are all connected to. What a beautiful concept.

Life events can tend to diminish our ability to remain connected to that eternal wisdom, to that plane of everlasting unconditional love also commonly referred to as Source or the Higher Mind. Access to that space can be regained through regular meditation, through regularly lifting the mind from the heavy burdens of the human experience, and through disconnection from the ego. Any time you get an inexplicable feeling or premonition, your higher self is trying to communicate with you. That feeling is your guide, steering you toward the best course of action.

Those who are primarily clairvoyant and clairaudient will gain the most benefit from doing this meditation, as it's quite often that symbols, channeled messages, or images regarding what must be done or changed about the current circumstances come into the inner eye and inner hearing. However, it is worth noting that connecting with the higher self is beneficial for everyone, as it affords a greater space of tremendous objectivity and freedom from the burdens the human ego imposes on the mind. It promotes self-acceptance and self-love.

The chakras that assist in your connection with your higher self are your seventh or crown chakra, your sixth or third eye, and your heart or fourth chakra. It is the combined effort of the crown to connect with the divine, the third eye's ability to bring in symbols and images, and the fourth to verify through a deeply compassionate response to your own human experiences. You will soon see in the meditation that focusing on opening the heart enhances the ability to connect more easily with higher-self wisdom.

In advance of this meditation, gather the tools and items for your own ritual that allow you to feel those chakras open and flowing. If you have an amethyst for opening the third eye or a clear quartz crystal for clarity, either would be a lovely addition to this meditation to enhance the connection with your higher self. When you are in a space of genuine connection, especially the first few times, this meditation may elicit strong emotion, which is perfectly normal. It is the way for the soul and spirit to move through the pain of the human experience and to begin to release what needs to be cleansed and healed.

The more you meditate to connect to your higher self, you can count on the time coming when you will have merged and become one with that part of yourself. Yes, there are times when you still will feel fatigued and slightly disconnected, but with a simple thought and moment of silence, you can instigate that reconnection quite simply.

Following is a list of ways in which you may know that you are merging with your higher self:

- Things seem to "click" for you on a regular basis.
- You have a strong sense of life purpose.
- You feel connected to your soul family.
- Synchronicities happen more often.
- Feeling a deeper sense of gratitude.
- You embrace both your dark and light sides, not feeling trapped by your shadow.
- You can get on a deep level there is more to the universe than meets the eye.
- Feeling more self-love.
- Harmonious relationships.

- No guilt or shame around setting firm boundaries.

- You find more humor about life.

- You feel more gratitude for what you do have.

CONSIDER THIS

Tuning into your higher self is like offering yourself a bird's-eye view of your own life, challenges, joys, and struggles. When you afford yourself the chance to momentarily step out of the life issues you are facing and whatever's at the forefront of your conscious mind, you have access to something more pure and beautiful: a deep compassionate well of understanding for the human struggle. For a moment, the struggle or issues no longer consume you, as you can get momentary respite.

The number one tip I give everyone to connect with your higher self is to do the things that make you feel the most relaxed. Get a massage, take a nap, rest, take a hot bath, read, listen to soothing music, watch a feel-good movie, disconnect and unwind, and meditate. You have 24/7 access to your higher self because it's part of you. Our busy lives keep us somewhat at a disadvantage and disconnected from that higher part of ourselves, so carving out space to provide an opportunity to feel connected is important.

This particular meditation came to me during a pivotal and extremely experimental time in my life, well over twenty years ago. It was the first time I realized (quite by accident) that I was capable of opening my own psychic gifts naturally to receive messages and guidance on my own life path. It was startling and beautifully moving, which is why I want to share it with you.

Most of my present-day practices and tools for development came out of the free reign I offered myself in the beginning for exploration and experimentation. It is not a mistake or wasted time to afford yourself the same freedom to explore.

As for the following meditation, its bonus appears afterward. You may feel less of the heightened emotion your current life situation is bringing about. Another common result of doing this meditation is calming intense current emotional responses, helping you face whatever it is you are dealing with in your life from a more centered space. It is especially powerful to do during transitional times in your life: facing an empty nest, career or job changes, home moves, changes in relationships, large purchases, financial decisions of any kind, seeing your parenting more clearly, evaluating the handling of a particular situation more clearly. It is impossible to overuse this meditation; it can become a part of your regular daily spiritual or meditative practice.

The first step is to sit in a quiet reflective state for a few moments, and bring a question to mind for your own life path. Wonderful questions for this meditation are: "What do I need to know now," "How can I best move through this issue," or "What is the next step," all the way to something much more specific such as what to change to feel more peace and joy in your life, a relationship, your career, or a decision you are currently making. If you don't have any current questions for your life path, you are best served by going into this meditation with some kind of intention. Suggestions include: feeling more calm and peaceful, understanding a situation more clearly, enhancing your own compassion, or receiving divine love and healing.

This meditation takes an average of fifteen to twenty minutes to complete. It can be done with or without soothing music, though if you do use music, songs without lyrics are best. If you don't currently have music for meditation, search on YouTube for plenty of options. (My personal favorite is Steven Halpern.)

Be sure you are sitting in a chair that you can easily get up and move behind. Sit comfortably with both feet on the ground. The time you take to do the initial portion of the meditation should not take long, a few minutes at most. Once you do this meditation from beginning to end a few times, you may alter it as you see fit, to include more time grounding and centering, simply allowing your spirit to lead the way.

MEDITATION

Begin by bringing your attention to your breath. Focus on the air moving in and out of your body, bringing your breath to a slower, more even pace. Once you feel grounded and centered, move your awareness to your heart center, right in the middle of your chest. Focus for a few moments on opening your heart.

Imagine ocean waves of healing light repeatedly pouring through your back, opening your heart wider and wider out the front of your body. Those ocean waves of light expand out into space, spreading out wider with each breath.

Feel an emerging sense of peace and calm with each breath, moving your heart energy outward, growing and expanding. Your heart is a powerful generator for inspired and loving guidance. Feel now a growing sense of compassion for yourself and others, as if your heart was reaching out in a healing embrace, sending love to all the nooks and crannies, the uncomfortable spaces, to those who are suffering. It simply requires a simple intention in a heart-opened space.

This is the time to state your intention for protection. You may invite your spiritual guides to surround you with a barrier of protection, or you may simply imagine a bright bubble of light surrounding your body. Use any color that inspires you: white (spiritual purity), pink (love), blue (spiritual awareness), or any color that inspires you is perfectly fine. Imagine your spiritual guides painting a golden translucent wall of protection all around you. Each stroke of their paintbrush secures your energy field, making you feel safe.

Gently open your eyes now, and slowly move to stand behind your chair. Once there, close your eyes and adjust to the new position. Rest your hands on the back of the chair. You are now in the position of the higher self. With your eyes closed, see your human self still sitting in the chair. Take this moment in and allow yourself to slowly become aware of that human's life experiences. Take it in, allowing any feelings, impressions, and insights to surface.

At this moment, you may depart from your original question, as thoughts and feelings overwhelm you, taking over the initial question and moving you instead into a total space of compassion and love for the self. Follow the instinct to move where the meditation takes you. Allow what is needed to surface without editing.

Your question now surfaces in your mind. Be present to what you are feeling, seeing, noticing. It may be subtle; just a slight shift in perspective, or it may be specific, with certain symbols or images coming to your mind. There is no single way to receive through this meditation. You may feel a powerful surge of emotion and that is all, or you may hear words. You may even have a deep inner knowing or you may be given a series of images. Take all the time you need, and when you feel the process is complete, come around the chair and sit back down.

Take a moment to breathe and release any unwanted energies down your grounding chords. Come back into your body, and spend time integrating your higher self with your human self in whatever way feels appropriate to you.

Sense the waves of energy that so beautifully opened your heart center coming back closer to your body, so that your heart doesn't stay so wide-open after completing this exercise. Open your eyes and journal the insights, images, feelings, and experiences you had. Allow yourself to take a few minutes to be in the power of your new awareness.

Helpful Guidance: Experiment with different heights when you stand up. Stand on a bed with the chair on the floor in front of you, or try standing at the top of a flight of stairs with the chair at the bottom. See how your perception changes.

FOR YOUR JOURNAL

How did it feel in the moment you were in the position of your own higher self? What messages, thoughts, impressions, images came to you during this meditation?

THIRTEEN

Psychic Tools

Incorporating psychic tools into a development practice can enhance what is already received naturally. No matter how we receive, all of us can benefit greatly by learning about and adding additional ways to receive information. It affords you the opportunity to develop a well-rounded practice, and, if offering your gifts to others, can provide a beautiful holistic experience for those you serve.

I encourage you to choose a few tools that speak to you, and then spend time in a deep dive, thoroughly learning about those. Some take more time to learn than others; however, the general rule of thumb is to choose the ones you feel the most called to. After my first astrology reading in 2000, I was so emotionally connected to its insights that I felt an overwhelming desire to learn more and have been studying astrology ever since. I discovered as time passed that astrology afforded me an avenue of deep exploration into the nature of the human psyche, archetypes that were presented as planets, and to making the connections with those planets to what was happening in the lives of my clients. The intense years of study combined with esoteric knowledge allowed me to enhance my offerings, and give in ways to my clients that regular readings couldn't. It added a layer of value, and often confirmed and validated things I saw with my inner vision.

My other favorite tool is tarot cards. I have been mesmerized with them ever since someone at a party nearly twenty years ago read my cards and told me things about myself she couldn't have possibly known. It is hard to believe I have been exploring and reading the cards for others ever since, but they have been such a wonderful source of support to what I naturally receive through my psychic gifts.

Your tool belt may end up being a bit different than mine. I encourage you to explore here and reflect on whatever else you might feel drawn to. The list is broken down alphabetically, and the dots have been connected for you so you don't need to wonder what sort of tools may best fit your own natural psychic gifts.

PSYCHIC TOOLS

Astrology: Astrology is a symbolic language that reveals the cosmic connection to the planets' rotation in the night sky. Astrologers help others understand their own charts, based on when and where they were born. An astrology chart can help someone understand their personality and temperament, also revealing the potential for a person's life, attitudes, and behaviors. In addition, certain types of astrology can help a person understand their own spiritual path and psychic abilities. This is an extraordinary and rather intensive study that easily can last a lifetime. There is an abundance of information to learn about the planets and signs. Most astrologers comment that they were called to learn and make use of this tool to help themselves and others. All "clairs" can benefit from learning astrology.

Breathwork: Breathwork is simply a practice of using the breath for healing. There are many different modalities and techniques. It involves using the breath in a consistent and rhythmic way for a certain period of time to achieve a euphoric state of mind, to release and heal from trauma, and to receive insights and information that are helpful to the breathwork practitioner. I highly encourage you to find a breathwork professional in your area who can facilitate a breath journey with you as a starting point. Those who are connected to the body—earth signs and water signs in particular—can benefit tremendously from using breathwork to assist in their own psychic development and personal growth.

Crystal ball: Gazing into a crystal ball, also known as scrying, has been around for hundreds of years. Scrying is the use of an object for focusing the attention, thereby opening the third eye and inner vision to receive insights and information. A crystal ball can assist someone who is clairvoyant or claircognizant to focus their sight for swift and accurate results. A practitioner can use any method for focusing the attention, not just crystal—a pond, bowl of water, fire, candle flame, or other object that transfixes the gaze may be used.

Grounding: While we explored this topic earlier in this book, it is worth noting its importance here, as it is an essential part of any psychic development toolbox. All the "clairs" can greatly benefit from this activity, as it roots the energies of the physical body so the sixth sense can expand freely and safely do its work. Hands-in-the-ground gardening, walking barefoot in the grass, hugging a tree, or meditation can all be appropriate ways to ground.

I-Ching: Also known as the *Book of Changes*, this ancient text has served for thousands of years as a philosophical exploration of the universe. It is a manual of sorts for us to understand ethical living; in ancient China, it was used as a manual for emperors, and it also served as an oracle for their personal future and the future of the realm. Competing schools of thought have muddied its use, unfortunately, but intense study of this ancient tool is still capable of opening doorways of understanding that some say explain everything. Even today in China and East Asia, the *I-Ching* remains by far the most consulted of all books for divinatory purposes.

Numerology: Numerology is the study of numbers as they relate to one's own life. People use numerology to gain understanding of their own life path, what qualities they exhibit that may help or hinder them, and to understand numbers and how they relate to the cycles of life, which are always changing. If you love to study, you will enjoy learning about this wonderful tool for enhanced awareness. Anyone can learn numerology and incorporate it in their own psychic practice.

Pendulum: A pendulum is any object that dangles from a string or chain used to measure energy. In a manner similar to dowsing rods, a pendulum measures the intensity of energies around you, and it can also help you distinguish which choices and decisions are best for you. People who are clairsentient (or water and earth signs) connect easiest to this particular tool. When used properly, pendulums can grant instant understanding regarding what may aid in the path of healing (much like applied kinesiology, a form of muscle testing).

Runes: These stones contain an ancient, magical alphabet, the glyph on each rune corresponding with a particular message. They have many uses, one of which is receiving messages and understanding this current life; the other is for divination or predicting the future. The root of the word *rune* means "secret" or "something hidden," indicating the important powers they hold. Anyone may use runes easily as a tool for their own personal psychic practice or to read for others.

Stones and crystals: Clairsentients (earth and water signs in particular) tend to be particularly drawn to including stones and crystals in their psychic development practice. Certain stones and crystals can be quite beneficial to opening psychic abilities, as stated in the earlier chapter on nature. Incorporating this as a tool into your own spiritual or psychic development practice increases your own natural gifts.

Cards–tarot, oracle, angel: The use of cards of any kind to read people, situations, or circumstances; gain advice; or tell futures is known as cartomancy. Some people enjoy the traditional tarot card deck, and others prefer a regular playing card deck, which can be read in a similar way, where each card number and suit has a particular meaning. Oracle and angel card decks have grown in popularity over the years as another way to gain important and relevant insight and receive messages. Those who aren't naturally clairaudient (clear hearing) may enjoy the use of cards as a tool, as they add layers of information to any reading. Those who see spirits as mediums but struggle to receive messages may find that including cards is a helpful way to connect with the spirit.

Visualization: This technique is similar to meditation, in that it is a tool that directs the mind in a particular way to achieve a specific outcome. Visualization techniques bring about a state of mental freedom, for the mind to direct the third eye to explore and receive without the burden of the ego. This is much easier for the clairvoyant; however, following a guided visualization can bring those in the other "clair" camps tremendous peace, as it's like listening to a story where you get to decide the plot and the outcome. People report feeling a deep sense of peace and serenity through the use of different visualization techniques.

No matter what psychic tools you choose to explore, they will greatly add to your own psychic development practice. However, they are not intended to take away from your own natural gifts. So as long as you use them in a fashion that supports your personal growth, you won't be in danger of using them as a crutch. Remember that these tools should support your natural gifts, not replace them.

FOURTEEN

Interpreting Psychic Messages

Psychic messages aren't always straightforward, sometimes causing confusion. When you receive a message that isn't clear, it means nothing about your psychic abilities. We don't always grasp or make sense of psychic information right away. This is actually a sign to you that the information is of a psychic nature. If you understand everything that comes to you in a psychic message right away, it's likely that the messages are coming more from your left brain than your right brain, which connects you to your intuition and sixth sense. When you do the meditations in this book, you will be developing your psychic skills so they become stronger, and you will also experience various psychic phenomena. Remember that it's not always possible to rationally understand what you receive. The knowing of the message comes in time with reflection and dedication to recognizing patterns.

The more you practice in development, the more quickly the understanding will come to you regarding the information and messages you are receiving. As your gifts grow, so will your ability to more quickly decipher the messages. The understanding often comes in accordance with a timing we do not get to control. When you can let go, release the messages, and aren't thinking about them anymore, this will allow you to release the waiting or holding onto the energy of wanting the answer. When you are less fixated or attached to receiving immediate understanding of what you are receiving, you can ease your left-brain thinking mind. The psychic messages and answers will slip in much more naturally.

It's important to understand that psychic information and messages are not consumed by the ego. They more so tend to float in effortlessly. When you receive a psychic impression for yourself or others, it will float in without difficulty. I typically instruct my own psychic boot camp attendees to practice receiving messages abundantly, until they are no longer emotionally attached to how the messages come in, or what those messages are. Real psychic messages aren't attached to any outcome; they enter on a stream of unbiased and peaceful presence. It is your job to remain undisturbed by your own beliefs or thoughts. It takes time and diligence, but you can do it.

When psychic downloads happen void of emotion, it can feel like we are missing something or doing it incorrectly. However, what is unique about the messages is that there is a back-end sense of certainty, peace, and calm, as well as the occasional surge of passion and excitement. They are energy-filled insights and don't cause harm or alarm to the one bringing them in.

They can arrive in a scattered moment and not make any sense. Developing psychic skills requires an ability to notice and live life simultaneously without harboring any intensity and angst around what, when, or how you receive. The more you can balance life and your sixth-sense notions, the easier it will become over time to tap into your psychic gifts.

Psychic messages can often motivate you into taking some sort of action. That doesn't necessarily mean the course of action leads to exact outcomes or even the outcome you wanted. Sometimes the outcome is unknown, but you must pull yourself toward it and move yourself out of your current conundrum or dissatisfied state by following through with that action. Insight paired with action over time creates desired results and changes in your life and the lives of others.

Our ego can be quite good at occasionally tricking us into thinking what we are experiencing is a legitimate psychic message, when in fact it is our imagination running wild. This is one of the most commonly asked questions I receive as a mentor. This practice on one hand requires surrendering to the process and on the other hand requires discernment. Here are some hints that you might be too rooted in your left brain and are not receiving accurate psychic information:

- The information presents in a string of thoughts that appear on a linear timeline. Psychic messages tend not to have any regard for time.

- Feeling stuck or overly emotional tends to pull you out of your psychic abilities and is a clear sign you are not accessing psychic information.

- Insights and messages reinforce what you already know to be true. Psychic information comes whether or not you know anything about the subject or topic being asked of you.
- If there is no originality to the information, it is probably not coming from your psychic gifts. Psychic information is largely surprising and unexpected.

It takes a willingness and diligence to remaining neutral, objective, and unbiased when channeling psychic messages, symbols, or information. That is why many psychics prefer focusing a portion of their practice on using their specific clair to bring in symbols. When bringing in symbols, we can get some distance from our common-sense, left-brained selves.

Repetitive messages, symbols, and signs are definitely something to pay attention to and notice; they are spirit's way of attempting to reach you with information of a significant nature to help you or someone else. As you go back through the meditation journaling exercises you did in this book, underline the repetitive themes and information/messages. That's where the important messages reside.

DECIPHERING PSYCHIC PHENOMENA

The range of psychic information people receive is vast. The list that follows is in no way comprehensive; to learn more about the symbols, signs, and messages you receive, check out the bibliography for additional resources.

Animals: Dragonflies, butterflies, cardinals, and feathers are most often a hello from a loved one who has crossed over.

Birth: Don't assume that seeing or dreaming about a baby being born means you'll have a baby. This more often is a symbol for something that is birthing: an idea, project, spiritual awakening, or significant change.

Colors: Gifted psychics and empaths can see patterns of color around a person, helping them understand what might be happening in the body, the aura, the mind, depending on where the color is located around the person.

Feathers: Connection with a loved one who has crossed over.

Flashing lights: Loved ones who have crossed over enjoy contacting us through paranormal phenomena such as lights turning on and off.

Numbers: Repeating numbers in multiples—such as 11:11, 222, 33, or any combination of the same ones are often a divine link to angelic support, guidance, and encouragement.

Smells: Scents, perfume, or cooking food without an apparent source are all signs of a nearby loved one.

Sparkling lights: Seen with your own physical eyes, this phenomenon is a direct link to spiritual guides.

Song lyrics: This is one of my favorite signs—when I have a question or want guidance from spirit, the first song I hear when I turn on the radio has a message for me.

Water: Visions or images that include water point to intense emotional disturbances and a need for addressing/healing emotional trauma.

FIFTEEN

Spirit Guide Meditation

The main helper from the spirit world in each of our lives is known as a spirit guide. Each of us has at least one and sometimes more than one. Spirit guides are entities or energy beings that may be called upon at any time for assistance, guidance, and comfort. Sometimes they are spirits you were connected to from past lifetimes, other times they are deceased loves ones, or they may be spirits you have never met before—it is different for everybody.

Each guide comes to you for a specific purpose, which is why you may have more than one. For example, one may be working with you on your creative gifts, another for healing physical body issues, and yet another for spiritual development. A spirit guide can also come to your assistance and intervene to help you during an accident by entering your body to communicate or stopping time. You can use your guide or guides to assist in delivering messages of encouragement to others, or to empower your own life choices.

Because we have free will, our spirit guides must be invited to participate in our lives. While they are always keeping the porch light on for us, they don't interfere arbitrarily—they need our permission. Thus, sometimes it takes years for people to meet their own personal guides; all that's actually needed is a simple introduction! It is sufficient to open your heart to them and welcome them in on a regular basis. Just let them know you are always interested in connecting with them.

Ways to know your spirit guide is connecting with you:

1. You see repetitive numbers in sequence.
2. You occasionally notice floating white or blue pin pricks of light around you.
3. You sometimes hear the cosmic hum, a ringing out of the blue in one of your ears.
4. Sometimes you'll hear a soothing voice in your head that does not sound like you.
5. Sensations of a presence followed by intense calm.
6. Your own inner knowing.

All the clairs are capable of connecting to spirit guides. Those who are clairsentient (feeling) and claircognizant (knowing) commonly feel warmth or a supportive presence around them. You are encouraged to have a deck of oracle or tarot cards handy so you can receive messages from your guides when you draw them close to you. Chapter 13 explores the use of oracle or tarot cards for retrieving messages from loved ones in spirit or spirit guides in more depth. Exercises for opening and clearing the second, third, and fourth chakras are a perfect foundational support for enhancing the connection.

Those who are clairaudient (hearing) or clairvoyant (seeing) will often receive words of guidance and encouragement during pivotal moments and decisions. Clairvoyants also may see color, light, or the outline of a physical form with their inner vision. Working on clearing and opening chakras five, six, and seven assists with this activity. For that reason, the chakra meditation on page 69 is an excellent companion to this chapter. Try doing those one after another for enhanced results.

Above all, no matter how you receive as a psychic, the important relationship between you and your spirit guide(s) does not discriminate. Although it may take you a while to feel confident in your connection with them, they are ready and willing, and will work with your own personal hardwiring. The time it takes to feel certain of your connection is also different depending on the person.

There are multiple ways to connect with your spirit guide, the first being through meditation. It feels so good to connect with their good intentions for you, feel their loving, warm presence. You may also connect with them through the use of a pendulum, tarot, or oracle cards. Try automatic writing, or ask them to show you signs and synchronicities to verify their presence. Invite them to enter your dreams when you go to bed at night. Before you start your day the next morning, spend time reflecting on the dream and how any symbols and messages are relevant to you. Hearing their messages coming through the lyrics of a song on the radio, on the television, or even on the license plates of cars on the road in front of you are all ways in which they will attempt reach you if you want them to.

If you desire a stronger connection, stay open. I have overheard conversations between people at my local coffee shop that validated something I was personally going through that answered a tough question. In fact, this sort of incident has happened so often that I now expect that from time to time I'm going to overhear something that helps me when I go there. Thanks to the consistency, my guides and I have established a clear pattern and way for them to deliver messages.

Make a list of your requests for help from your spirit guide. It is amazing what sorts of direct assistance shows up when we ask! An example: "Help show me the pathway to the best career path for my highest good," or "Help bring to me a love relationship that is for my highest good," or "Bring to me the best options for assisting my physical health issues." Your willingness to ask for their assistance will bring them closer to you. Then be ready to notice what is shifting around you—what opportunities are coming to you that weren't there before? Be willing to release any plans you had previously laid down for something that comes along that serves your path even better. It's just as important to avoid manipulating outcomes by resisting letting go of outworn ideas or plans. Accept that there may be an opportunity to change things.

CONSIDER THIS

Establishing your own personal relationship with your spirit guides is something you get the opportunity to develop over the entire course of your life, and everyone connects with their spirit guide differently. What I've discovered over the course of many years mentoring others is that sometimes you are invited to know them thoroughly: their name, personality, and how you were perhaps connected in a lifetime before this one. Other times, guide energies come through a feeling, such as a presence. The most common phenomena people experience to confirm their guides' presence are: tingling, warmth, the feeling of a presence behind them, vibrations in the third eye, a deep knowing, and even blissful tears. I have a client whose arm twitches when her guide is present. Another client channels her guides through automatic writing, and yet another feels their spirit guide coming through to them as if someone laid a warm blanket on their shoulders.

I believe that the "need" for our spirit guide to have a name or identity is largely on our part; supportive entities in the spirit realm do not need such things. The need belongs only to us as human beings and is largely a function of the ego's desire to engage in a relationship in a way which makes logical sense that our mind can accept and comprehend. If you are curious about something to do with your guides, just ask! Then let go and allow it to come to you as it can. As soon as all options are possible, you will likely break through this barrier, and it won't feel so frustrating when you aren't "seeing" or "hearing" your guide as your mind (that is, your ego) expects to see and hear it. Eliminate that need and you open up to a wider realm of possibility, where your guides can come through in exactly the way they are able to. Just embrace them and the notion that they are there, supporting and helping you.

The meditation in this chapter is a powerful way to connect with spirits because the first step is entering your own inner sanctuary. Your inner sanctuary is a sacred space where only those you invite to join may enter. In addition, it establishes a repetitive signal to guides that they may join you there when you are ready. Establishing a rhythmic pattern and somewhat predictable routine with your spirit guides sets a healthy tone for future interactions. Like a light switch, you are not required (nor is it recommended) to be perpetually "on." You are a human being with a life outside the one you share with the spirit realm, and let's face it—it's nice to interact and engage with people without the constant disruption of spirit. While in the beginning it can be exciting to hear, feel, and see messages from your spirit guide, the inclusion of the inner sanctuary creates a structure that respects your own space when not in direct contact. Over the years, I have found that it is critical to establish healthy boundaries with this kind of work.

Not only can your spirit guide offer you guidance and insights for your own life path, they also may act as a direct link for you to connect with loved ones in spirit for others. To this day I credit my own guides who call themselves "the Band of Light" for consistently opening my eyes to the beautiful, meaningful, and helpful messages for those I have served over the years. It is a sacred bond I cherish and hold dear.

This meditation takes fifteen to thirty minutes on average, depending on what you see, feel, sense. First, find yourself a quiet, dimly lit room. It's best to work alone without the distractions or disruptions of others. You may choose to have soft background music, though silence is also acceptable. Meditation for psychic development is truly an art form, one you will practice and refine over time.

As with all exercises and meditations, do what feels most natural to you.

MEDITATION

Close your eyes. Using your inner vision, look up at your pituitary gland, which is located behind the bridge of your nose. This area commands perception, knowledge, and authority. Its primal relationship is with inner and cosmic knowledge. Try to keep your eyes focused on this point. The muscles around your eyes may become sore as you stretch them upward; at first, don't overdo it. As you practice, this step will become easier.

As you focus on your third eye, imagine, sense, and feel you are standing on a grassy hill. Bring yourself to the very top of the hill. When you are ready to begin, walk down this hill. Notice, sense, and feel each step as you walk down the hill. Imagine yourself moving safely and with ease. Use all your senses to experience this descent. When you are walking along the bottom of the hill feeling very safe, see yourself healthy and carefree. Allow your sense of being to be part of this place as it fills your body and mind. Take a moment to imagine or sense it.

Somewhere nearby is a clear, still pond. As you approach the pond, notice a mist is forming near it. This mist hugs the earth. Intuitively, you are aware that your guide is approaching, inviting your soul into this realm of heightened awareness. Reach out your hand into the mist. Be aware of your guide's hand gently slipping into your own.

The mist begins to clear now, and you have the opportunity to meet, see, or sense your guide. You trust and know this is so. You may become aware of your guide's presence and appearance, or you may simply feel warmth or a comforting presence around you. If you are able, you may begin to distinguish your guide's physical appearance. However it appears to you is perfectly fine. Take it all in and be open to sense their good intentions and love.

Feel your guide's energy surrounding you both spiritually and physically. Now make a mental note of this feeling so that you can recognize it when you return from this meditation, thereby allowing you to sense your guide and subsequently connect with them during your day-to-day life, if appropriate. Greet your guide, and ask them if you once knew each other. They may or may not respond. Now is the time to insert a question for support or guidance. Trust what you receive, which may be a feeling or something more specific, like an image or symbol.

Invite your guide to give you a flower. They pick one from the grassy hillside and hand it to you. Flowers are often used as symbols and messages, depending on their type. If you don't know what kind of flower your guide has given you, that's okay.

Spend as much time as you wish in this space, and enjoy the feelings of deepening connection, love, and support for your life path. Reconnect with your breath, and take a moment to further deepen your sense of peace and relaxation.

It is time to conclude your visit. Thank your guide for coming into your awareness in whatever way feels appropriate. Say goodbye to them for now in a loving way that feels right. Watch as the mist forms again around them near the pond. Imagine yourself now moving back from the pond and the mist. Ascend the grassy hill once more. From there, your soul connects again with your physical body. As that happens, all the visions, sensations, answers, and gifts you might have received integrate with your conscious mind and are automatically stored there now for easy assimilation and access.

Helpful Guidance: Ponder and write down questions for loving guidance before beginning the meditation. After you have completed the meditation, research any symbols to decode the messages they are providing you during this time.

FOR YOUR JOURNAL

What did you see, feel, and/or sense from your spirit guides during this meditation? Were there any messages, guidance, colors, or symbols that came through?

SIXTEEN
Being in Nature Meditation

Nature serves as a temple unto itself. As humans, we receive pleasure from observing and connecting with its beauty. We also benefit greatly from understanding and cultivating deep awareness in our own lives, because nature itself shifts our own energy: we are able to open to the vastness of our inner selves through the vastness of the natural world.

Those who are empaths or clairsentient in particular can gain a tremendous amount of expansion in their innate psychic gifts from allowing their aura to commune with things living in our natural world. Connecting with the earth through a technique called earthing, getting hands in the dirt, or sitting in a quiet space under a tree, all grant the beneficial experience of merging the soul with nature, becoming one with all things. This relaxed space of contemplation is where the psychic abilities thrive. In addition to empaths, those who are earth signs (Taurus, Virgo, and Capricorn) can maximize the power of their own element to wake up the senses. Collaborative moments in nature spark and catalyze psychic abilities with ease. Being in the crisp air surrounded by the elements causes your conscious mind to become more alert, relaxed, and open to the abundance of messages this living world has to share with us. The opportunity exists in nature to quiet the mind, therefore connecting more deeply with the world around you. When we are open to it, there is a magical connection that naturally happens between each of us and the natural world.

A mysterious force that connects all living things, and the simple reminder of the complexity of the intricate systems that aid in keeping leaves on a tree alive, that allow new moss to grow, or that permit fruit to ripen, is miraculous. We are reminded also that we are only one minuscule part of this planet, a vast place of never-ending micro-relationships and life all around us. In addition, the intimacy we experience when a cardinal stops to say hello, or we stop to observe the intricate pattern of a spider web as if we've just been invited to dinner, or the quiet startle of making eye contact with an urban coyote, can move us out of the mundane self. You don't have to go deep into the wilderness to make contact with nature; your backyard will do.

Observing the natural world is a meditation in itself. There are reasons why spiritual gurus and wise teachers spend days in nature and require followers to do the same. Nature's soul-moving and healing potential exists for us every day. Unlike our mind, our body and senses are always in the present. Being present in nature makes it much easier for us to inhabit our body and the realm of the senses. And outside of our temperature-controlled houses, the natural world entices our senses to wake up. When we step outdoors, our skin receptors enliven as we feel subtleties of temperature and breeze. Our hearing becomes sharper as we listen to nuances of birdsong, silence, and the rustling of leaves. Most of all, our eyes become captivated by the beauty, texture, and sheer diversity of color, shape, and form.

NATURE'S HEALERS

For sensitive feelers who mainly receive through the hands, the heart, and solar plexus chakras, it is recommended to incorporate nature meditation into your spiritual practice. You are particularly hardwired to receive through the kinesthetic sensibilities and thus sense impressions from your surroundings through touch, feeling, and holding. Those with this sort of receiving capability typically do quite well with healing tools from the earth such as crystals and stones. Your crystal and rock shops will be a fantastic resource, as many of them have guidebooks in-house to help you determine what you need. As a general rule of thumb, the crystals or stones you feel drawn to are the ones you need. If you don't have local New Age bookstores or rock/crystal shops, you can still do a tremendous amount of research online. Here is a list of basic rocks/stones and their healing properties for your own personal use.

HEALING STONES AND CRYSTALS

Agate: Strength and courage

Amethyst: Calming and intuition

Angelite: Awareness

Aquamarine: Clarity and purification

Carnelian: Warmth, joy

Citrine: Revitalization, cleansing

Clear calcite: Cleansing

Clear quartz: Energizing

Fluorite: Focus and protection

Green aventurine: Emotional tranquility

Green jade: Emotional balance

Hematite: Protection and healing

Jasper: Balance and stability

Labradorite: Spiritual connection

Moonstone: New beginnings

Peridot: Compassion

Rose quartz: Love and peace

Selenite: Clarity of mind (also a wonderful stone for clearing energies the other crystals have gathered)

Smoky quartz: Clears blocked energy

Sodalite: Self-truth

Tiger's eye: Personal power

What sorts of messengers or messages can come to us from nature? Animals are one of nature's best messengers. Their presence across our path isn't coincidental. Notice what animals cross your path. When you are meditating outdoors, take note, and later research their meaning and message for your life. The following is a list of some of the most common spiritual animal messengers and a little bit about their messages.

COMMON ANIMAL MESSENGERS

Beaver: Ingenuity and persistence in work

Blue jay: Intelligence, determination, fearlessness

Butterfly: Connection with loved ones from the afterlife; transformation

Cardinal: Connection with loved one from the afterlife

Coyote: Surrender to the present moment

Crow: On the verge of manifesting what has been on your mind

Dragonfly: Connecting with the afterlife

Eagle: Renewed life; connecting with your spiritual path

Falcon: Victory, success, rising above challenging situations

Fox: The solution for the problem is within reach

Hawk: Use your intuition to make an important decision

Horse: Freedom; tending to your emotional, mental, and spiritual well-being

Raccoon: Surrender; letting go of a harmful situation or person

Snake: Rebirth, transformation, healing

Spider: Make use of your creativity to make beautiful things

Turkey: Celebrate resources and what you have; abundance

Wolf: Survival, self-confidence, courage

Stand close to a tree and touch it with your bare hand. The ancient wisdom held there can be heard, felt, and seen with your inner vision. Sit on the ground and move your bare feet through the grass. Feel the instant balancing the energy of the earth contributes to your own sense of well-being. Enhancing your well-being is the accelerator to opening your psychic abilities. Nature provides an incredibly supportive environment and atmosphere for expanding the capacity to receive.

Take a lunch break and go to a park. Sit under a tree on the ground, and lie on the grass, gazing up at the leaves. If you are an urban dweller, don't worry! This is a time to dig deep and be adventurous; learn about the sacred spaces around you. Churches and temples in your city typically have a green space. For free or at most a small donation, you can go to their garden and sit quietly. City parks are wonderful places to meditate. You can carve out a small area, have a picnic, and be in silence. Some building rooftops have garden spaces as well. Art museums in most cities have outdoor spaces where you can go to rest and relax. If you live near a college or university campus, you can find a quiet, grassy place. Do your research, and you'll soon have many options for connecting with nature.

Prepare a nature meditation tool kit and toss it in your car or front closet for easy access. In a backpack, include a small blanket or pillow, walking stick, a hat, sunscreen, a small notebook and pen, a snack, and any other ritual items you would like to have as part of your meditation. Just like other meditations, this one can be as elaborate or as simple as you'd like. If you feel like having precious crystals, stones, and gems handy to spread out around you, bring those. Let the sun bathe your stones and crystals for a nice recharge. If you are near water, you can give your ritual items a soak. Remember to include a small towel and a change of socks in case you are inspired to dip your toes. And though the items here listed can be part of ritual, don't forget the more practical items as well. For longer meditative walks and hikes out of town, be aware of what wildlife occupies those spaces, so you aren't surprised in the event of a bear sighting, for example.

For best results during this meditation, allow yourself to experience the sights, sounds, and smells without labeling them and becoming mentally involved with them. Notice the tendency of the mind to intellectualize and label everything: "Oh, look at that beautiful bird. What kind is it? Is it here all winter or where does it go?" When these kinds of thoughts come up, let them go. Notice without overanalyzing in the moment. Analysis can come later. For now, simply experience the colors, shape, sounds, movement of birds, the sky, or whatever else is around you. Allow it to be an experience that doesn't need to have significant meaning attached to it. Be mindful and present.

Sit quietly upright in a place where you feel safe being completely yourself. Easy spots for this are large boulders, a grassy patch under a tree, or even lying in the grass, as long as you are comfortable. If you are in a chair, sit free from the back of the chair to rest your feet on the ground.

MEDITATION

Close your eyes. Begin following your breath. Notice the inhalations and exhalations moving through your body. Feel your lungs rise and fall, the feeling of the air moving. Invite the breath into every cell of your being. The energy of your breath fills up every cell of your being. Do this for some time, as though your being were inhaling or drinking the spiritual energy around you. Be in a place of relaxed receptivity, not effort. Notice your body willingly receiving this nourishment.

Bring your attention to your root chakra, at the base of your spine, at your sit bones, your pelvic floor. Imagine, sense, and feel this area is part of the earth upon which you sit. You are now connected intimately with the earth's welcoming energies. Sense this energy coming to life within you. Open your heart in alignment and in harmony with the pulsing energies of the earth.

From this foundation, open your eyes and observe the sky, then the trees, then the other vegetation and life around you. Feel your body opening with joy, then ease, and then freedom. Notice the colors and fragrances; continue to tend to your breath, filling your entire body with this fresh newness and vitality.

Watch this vital energy rise above the tops of the trees and flowers and see within the trunks of the trees to the core of their own strength. Sense their good wishes. Listen to how the leaves rustle in the wind. Your senses stretch now, heighten, while you maintain your present rootedness to the earth.

Notice the tops of the trees and how they dance into the sky. Listen to the messages and stories from decades of growth, standing strong through the seasons' changes, providing homes for so many without complaint, without objection. Honor the tree with your silence. Close your eyes now; gratitude now flows through your heart and soul to the trees around you.

Let the birds, bugs, and wildlife catch your eye. Feel the freedom of the sky through your breathing now—the light, the expansiveness of it all, and the possibility rising up through the ground now to greet your heart.

In this fullness, notice your whole being merging with the entire universe, with everything that is. You are the world and the world is in you. Your body becomes a tree, joining in a celebration of life with the other trees around you. You are still, vast, stretching out, holding form without complaint, and rooted in the soil and open to the heavens. Rest in the fullness of who you are. Feel and allow every single cell in your body to resonate with the truth and the strength of your own infinite being.

Still rooted in the thick, moist soil through your pelvic floor, glance around and notice the clouds moving on a palette of blue, illuminated by the sun's rays. See what patterns and shapes they make, the messages they transfer to you through their own artistry.

The air is your breath. You feel its energy moving through you, the energy that generates healing, grounding, and release. You express a moment of gratitude for the moment to breathe in and feel the breeze or wind circulating around you. Notice what messages you hear floating on the breeze. Allow them to come into you. Feel, sense, or hear them and accept their wisdom.

It is time now to give back. Imagine your entire body becoming one with the natural surroundings. You are fully in communion with everything, and you exchange good intentions for continued growth and healing for the environment and Mother Earth. You release your own love and good intentions for all living things deep into the ground and see the waves of light on your inner eye as they move outward, sending their healing support to wherever it is needed.

Take all the time you wish to be in this harmonious place of communion.

Bring movement slowly back to your body. Take a few long breaths and open your eyes.

Helpful Guidance: Find a place in nature with little to no traffic noise. I find it exciting to try out different locations. Remember to prepare for whatever the elements are. Try meditating in a hammock—it's amazing.

FOR YOUR JOURNAL

How does being in nature impact your own sense of awareness? What are the places you can go outdoors to explore for your next meditation? Make a list.

SEVENTEEN
Auras and Energy Meditation

The aura is the invisible electromagnetic field that exists around your body, and everyone has an aura. Physics tells us everything has energy, and so everything also has an aura. Have you ever had the experience of being in a room where someone walks in and immediately radiates a larger-than-life energy? You are experiencing their aura, and this phenomenon is actually more accurate than you would think. The aura behaves like a balloon: sometimes the balloon has little air in it and is therefore a bit closer to the body, typically during times when one is melancholic, ill, sad, and closed off or isolated from the world. At other times, the balloon is fully inflated, especially during times of happiness, joy, and when you are feeling fully able to express yourself and vibrant.

There are seven auric layers that exist around our bodies: physical, astral, lower, higher, spiritual, intuitional, and absolute planes. Each layer correlates with different aspects of your spiritual, mental, and physical health. The one that psychics, seers, and healers tend to deal with the most is the physical auric field. Those who are clairsentient and claircognizant often easily sense the aura and are able to manipulate energy with their own hands. Reiki healers, energy workers, and massage therapists often sense the aura and what needs cleansing and healing energy that is channeled through their hands.

The most common way an aura's colors are revealed is through your inner vision. It's not something typically viewed with your physical eyes; it is instead reflected on your own inner vision, or inner knowing.

For the purpose of this exercise and meditation, we aren't focusing on one particular layer. In the beginning, an aura can appear within your inner vision or inner knowing as a swirling, slow-moving cyclone of energy containing a mixture of color and symbols. For now, it's not important to know which layer is more afflicted than the others. As you further develop your own psychic abilities, you may discover your own inner vision showing you many more of the distinct and separate layers over time. What's most important is to experiment (as much as your comfort allows) with seeing and feeling the aura, and then gathering information from it to support your own healing path and the healing of others. Just like with the chakras, there is a wealth of understanding and awareness to be gained regarding what is going on in the more subtle energy fields that rotate around the body in space as clues to the person's spiritual, emotional, and physical health.

CONSIDER THIS

You have a tremendous sense of control over your own aura because it is energy that resides in space around your physical body. Close your eyes for a moment and get a sense of where your aura is located around your body. Is it close to you or further away? Trust your first impression. Notice how you are feeling emotionally at the moment. Now think about something that makes you feel happy, and feel or watch your aura expand with your inner vision. Now bring to mind something that makes you feel sad. Feel your aura constricting, or drawing closer to your body. When you close down emotionally, your aura naturally closes in to protect you. When you feel lively and free, your aura is expansive and positively affects those around you. Notice how your electromagnetic field shifts depending on your own mood or thoughts in the present moment.

Through our aura, we affect those around us. When you adjust your own energy field and expand or contract your own aura, you gain the power to navigate difficult or uncomfortable social experiences. When in a busy, crowded space, try expanding your aura. Feel yourself filling up the space you are in, shielding yourself from the overwhelming energies around you. You can find a tremendous sense of instant peace and calm in those moments. If you are at an uncomfortable social gathering and don't want to be noticed, try contracting your auric field with your mind—do you notice others' attention toward you dissipate?

Keep the aura clean and clear of energetic clutter on a regular basis. There are many ways to cleanse the aura. You can move your hands in a sweeping motion in the space around your body, as if you are ironing out your own energy field with your hands. Burning incense, or sacred herbs such as sage, around your body and space is an automatic aura-balancing technique. The burning of the herbs or incense creates a cloud of smoke you can move around your body to cleanse it or clear and purify your living space. Light the plant material of your choice and blow out the flame. It will begin to smolder. While moving the smoke around your body, say a prayer or mantra, for example, "I am cleansed of anything that no longer serves me."

Here are the benefits of regular aura cleansing:

1. To clear energy blockages that can trigger illness.

2. To improve your mental and emotional well-being.

3. To let go of past conflicts and emotional distress.

4. To process and release negative energy.

5. To open yourself energetically to the abundant blessings of spiritual healing.

6. To protect yourself from being overly influenced by the emotions of others.

The color in your aura is indicative of your spiritual, physical, or emotional health, as well as your personality. You generally have one or two colors that are fairly consistent in your own aura, but those colors can change and other colors can be added, depending on what is currently going on in your own life. Colors may be dull or bright, which can have significance in how you are feeling or what is happening mentally, emotionally, and spiritually.

An easy way to use this aura colors chart is to notice during the meditation which colors you see, feel, or know; do your best to pay attention to whether whatever color you are sensing is a softer version of that color or a brighter tone. As a general rule of thumb, the brighter the color, the healthier the aura. The softer or more faded colors means that it's not as strong as it could be and therefore could definitely benefit from some healing through meditation or aura cleansing.

BASIC AURA COLORS CHART

Red: Passion, raw emotion, willpower, survival

Blue: Spiritual wisdom, calm energy, loving, sensitive, intuitive

Green: Connection with nature, healing energy, love of people, giver

Orange: Maternal instincts, caregiver, outgoing, social, confidence, courageous

Yellow: Awakening, inspiration, intelligent, creative, playful, optimistic, easy-going

Purple: Intuitive, visionary, futuristic, idealistic, artistic, magical

Pink: Compassion, loving, tender, nonjudgmental, creative

White: Spiritual purity, connection with the divine

Gold: Spiritual protection, angels hovering close by

The following meditation can take anywhere from five to twenty minutes, depending on your aura's health. If you wish, supplementing this meditation with soft music can greatly enhance the relaxation and ease with which you can tune in to or sense the colors and information that live there.

MEDITATION

This is a meditation that supports both sitting-up and lying-down postures. Choose the one that makes you feel the most comfortable. Begin by focusing on your breath, moving the air in through your nose and out through your mouth. Feel the cares and concerns from your day dissipating with each breath and allow your inner chatter to fade into the background. Invite your guide to join you for this meditation to assist and facilitate any additional support, insight, or wisdom.

As your breath slows to a steady, even pace, release any tension you are carrying in your head, neck, shoulders, and jaw. Feel the smooth and deep release of that energy to a much softer, more natural rhythm. As you continue to breathe at an easy pace, sense the presence of the bioenergetic life force within you. Imagine and feel this energy flowing through you, cleansing you from the inside out. Visualize this energy within your body radiating more and more. See if you can see/sense the color of the energy.

Direct any healing color or energy to any places in your body where you feel pain or concern. Feel the healing release deep into your tissues, organs, bones, and cells.

Now turn your attention to the etheric field outside of your body. Notice and feel how it rotates around your body, always moving, alive, and carrying in it information, color, and symbols. Take in what colors and information are there, letting go of the need to analyze them for now. Just be present to what you see, sense, and feel.

Continue to feel your energy body around you. Now notice if you can see any murky areas, holes, tears, rips, or sections of grainy energy located there. Invite your guides, angels, and healing beings of light to come near you now and assist with the process of healing and repairing your aura. You are only calling upon those beings who are from the light, coming forward in the highest expression of unconditional love. You may now move your hands around your body to smooth out your aura, assisting with healing any small holes or tears. The energy beings are there to assist, and they are experts at strengthening your energy field. By asking them to come, you are granting them permission to assist you in attaining instant healing energies.

Stop for a moment and just be. Feel and sense how your auric field is feeling, and take note of anything else that may be needed right now. Invite any other healing beings of light to further assist you, knowing that whatever you need will be provided. You reach out with an open heart and ask for additional deepening of this aura-mending process. Express your gratitude for the beings of light coming forward to assist you now.

Now or very soon, you may even observe or notice those beings of light and how they are assisting with your aura-healing and mending process. Pay close attention to what physical sensations you feel as this healing process continues and deepens even further. What are you seeing, sensing, hearing, or feeling right now that is needed to continue to heal after this meditation? Be open to words of encouragement and messages of continued support.

The number of times a week to do this meditation depends on how you feel about your energy. You may use this meditation when you feel your energy levels are low or even when you're simply feeling down or in a funk. Daily cleansing through these techniques affords you the chance to rid yourself of negative energies you've picked up from your environment and others. It increases your own energetic vibrational frequency.

Helpful Guidance: Use this aura meditation often. It is one that benefits both the spiritual and physical body.

FOR YOUR JOURNAL

What colors did you see, sense, or feel in your own aura? Based on the aura colors chart, what did you learn about yourself?

EIGHTEEN
Dreamwork Meditation

When you go to sleep at night, the line between the physical and spiritual world dissolves, and your soul has the ability to travel beyond the conscious world. Your soul knows no limits, and if offered the chance, will delight in being set free to explore. If the conditions are just right, you may connect with loved ones or spiritual guides, travel to other dimensions and realms, and receive messages from beyond. You can interpret the meaning of dreams to change your core beliefs, relationships, hopes, and fears. The more importance you place on your dreams, the more you will remember, and the easier it will be to interpret your dreams every day.

Using your dream state to achieve a deeper understanding of yourself to heal emotional trauma and receive messages of guidance and support from the spirit world is called dreamwork. Everyone dreams, but not everyone is able to remember their dreams. I often inform my clients that even if they don't recall their dreams, they are still having them and those dreams are still working to help them heal on their behalf. Those who have highly active imaginations/creative minds are more likely to dream and remember their dreams.

If you are clairvoyant or clairaudient, it may be easier for you to experience and recall the messages, stories, and symbols the next day. Those messages, stories, and symbols can offer important clues to what is being communicated to you from the spirit world, or what needs healing on a subconscious level. Those who are primarily clairsentient and claircognizant may not recall dreams but will feel viscerally changed in some way by what happened during their sleep travels. They may feel more emotionally charged, and know something shifted inside them during sleep.

Stimulate a more functional dream state by working on the meditation for activating your third eye from this book, the meditation for clairvoyance chapter, and clearing your fifth, sixth, and seventh chakras on a regular basis. What you have on your mind when you go to bed can greatly influence your dreams, so it is wise to clear your mind before bed.

Have you ever noticed that sometimes you wake up from a dream and the symbols and happenings appear so random, you have absolutely no idea what they are trying to tell you? When you dream, the unconscious mind takes over. Your unconscious mind presents in primitive feelings and urges, sort of like a toddler. There is no logic involved, and dreams don't have linear timelines or stored memories to lean upon. Your unconscious mind takes what it can grab from your imagination, in other words. So when the strange connections that don't make sense to the logical brain appear in your dreams, it is your more primitive unconscious mind holding the reins. If nothing else, it can be entertaining! If you can interpret those connections and apply their resulting insights to everyday waking life, you give yourself a powerful tool for understanding yourself.

So how do you know whether you are having a dream to help heal your subconscious mind versus a dream that is a psychic experience? The only way to really understand and analyze the difference is through dream interpretation. To begin your dream interpretation, first look for symbols. Start a dream journal and aim to write down at least one new dream per day.

In your dream journal, underline everything you think might be a dream symbol no matter how ridiculous it may sound, such as a pig riding a bicycle or a talking baby. Although illogical or nonsensical, these symbols have a deeper meaning to the unconscious mind. Next, ask yourself how you feel about what happened in the dream when you wake up. Following that, ask yourself what is currently going on in your life that would be represented by the story or symbols in your dream.

Also, please stay tuned to recurring dreams; their themes are often important clues regarding whatever you may be trying to heal or come to terms with. Recurring dreams can also serve as important messages that loved ones or spiritual guides are trying to share with you. One last important thing to note: dreams about death are rarely about an actual death, and more about the symbolism of death—transformation, endings, and new beginnings. In that instance, ask yourself what it is you have been fantasizing about ending—for example, a job, relationship, or pattern of behavior.

HOW TO INTERPRET DREAM SYMBOLS

The basis of dream interpretation is the identification of important dream symbols whose true meanings are then translated.

Some common themes and symbols are: water images (flooding or floating, sailing, being at sea), falling, being in an elevator going up, being in a car going fast or slow, being in a house (sometimes yours, sometimes someone else's), flying, or meeting up with loved ones who have crossed over. Other common themes are being lost somewhere without knowing how to get back, or reconnecting with long-lost lovers or friends and family.

The unconscious is taking a concept and showing it to you masked as a dream symbol. If you are soaring high and enjoying the landscape below, it is likely that you are in control of your life. However, if you are faltering or falling, your unconscious is telling you that you lack control or are vulnerable in life. Trees, power lines, buildings, or gravity may obstruct your flying dream. Pay attention to the symbols that stand out and notice how you interact or engage with those things. If you have recurring flying dreams like this, try to identify who or what is at the root of your fears. What in your life feels out of control? Intentional work around your dreams will empower you in your waking life. When you make necessary changes and work to heal and address the subconscious fears, you can move beyond whatever may be holding you back in life.

So don't rely on dream dictionaries exclusively, because there is no way that your mind conforms to all the same "dream rules" set by the author. You can become your own dream interpreter if you are willing to journal and watch for themes and patterns that emerge over time. That said, dream dictionaries can provide some value based on the fact that we have all grown up in the same culture, the same era, and we are all human. It's no coincidence that we can unconsciously make similar conclusions about life, and a dream dictionary makes a good starting point for the translation.

DREAM JOURNAL EXERCISE

What follows is a questionnaire you can use as a template when you wake up in the morning. It can help you decipher whether the dream you are having is based on something that is going on in your life or subconscious mind, or something that is coming through your sixth sense to be used as a psychic message.

1. What was the dream about?

2. How do you feel after waking up?

3. Describe any colors, symbols, backdrops, locations. Who were you with?

4. Does anything unusual or unique stand out to you from the dream?

5. What was the tone of the dream: exciting, terrifying, joyful, happy, sad, etc.?

6. What is happening in your current life that your dream might be helping reveal to you?

7. What could the dream be trying to help you heal?

8. What is the final message or takeaway from the dream? Was the dream healing something psychologically or connecting psychically?

DREAMWORK EXAMPLE

My client Judy connected with me after a powerful dream in order to understand the nature of the dream and whether or not it was a psychic experience or one to help her release and heal her psychological issues. Here's how I would use the list of questions to assist in understanding the deeper meaning of the dream.

1. What was the dream about?

   Judy entered a church. In the basement was a long dining table set for a meal. She sat down at the dining table, and her mother joined her for dinner. Suddenly her mother began talking about all the other loved ones in spirit who were also going to be joining them for dinner. Little by little, they also appeared.

2. How do you feel after waking up?

   Judy felt a combination of joy, sadness, and peace.

3. Describe any colors, symbols, backdrops, locations. Who were you with?

   The church initially appeared in her dream as if she had entered a black-and-white photo. She remembered the smell in particular, which was of an old dusty building. Also the church was in the town her mom grew up in; she recognized it from old pictures. Her mom and several other loved ones who had crossed over appeared.

4. Does anything unusual or unique stand out to you from the dream?

   The unusual or unique thing was that she hadn't thought of any of the other family members in the dream.

5. What was the tone of the dream: exciting, terrifying, joyful, happy, sad, etc.?
   The dream was joyful and exciting, sort of like a reunion.

6. What is happening in your current life that your dream might be helping reveal to you?
   No answer.

7. What could the dream be trying to help you heal?
   Connecting with loved ones who have crossed over.

8. What is the final message or takeaway from the dream?

This was definitely a psychic experience dream in which Judy was connecting with her family. The rather surprising aspects of the dream—visiting a place that appeared black-and-white and the family members she had not thought of in years coming into the dream—felt to her like a genuine connection.

NINETEEN
Mediumship Meditation

People who use their psychic abilities to connect with the world of spirits are known as mediums. When our physical body dies, the essence or energy, our life force, which some refer to as spirit, disperses. It is invisible to the naked eye and transfers into the astral plane. However, some have the ability to shift their awareness to connect with the astral plane and telepathically communicate with loved ones in spirit. The connection happens telepathically, mind-to-mind with the spirit realm.

If you consider yourself clairvoyant (clear seeing), clairaudient (clear hearing), or claircognizant (clear knowing), you may have the ability to easily see/sense and connect with loved ones who have crossed over. Remember, however, that not all psychic receivers receive in the same way. If you are clairsentient (clear feeling) you may also be able to connect, though it may come through an emotional reaction, a feeling surging through your body that develops at times when loved ones are close, rather than receiving an image or a message. You may feel them, see them, hear them, know they are present, or some combination. Do not worry or strain yourself to try too hard to experience a connection with them in any one particular way; instead, allow it to happen the way it's meant to for you. Before you embark on this exciting journey, I advise revisiting chapters 11 and 15, on grounding for protection and spiritual guides. The meditations in those chapters are perfect for laying the groundwork that allows you to explore connecting with loved ones in spirit.

Connecting with loved ones who have crossed over can be a profoundly sacred and healing moment; you get to experience a reunion, of sorts. This exercise can trigger more emotional reactions than the other exercises in this book, so this is definitely in the category of a more advanced psychic development skill. If you connected easily with spiritual guides and spirit animals, you may find you also have an easy time connecting with loved ones in spirit. It is remarkably rewarding and worth the effort.

TOOLS

During meditation, your analytical, logical mind takes a holiday, providing the perfect atmosphere to connect with spirit, unhindered. Because spirit communicates telepathically, you will not be able to easily connect if your mind is cluttered with thoughts or distractions.

There are several ways in which to connect to and receive messages using your mediumistic skills in addition to meditation. One of those ways is through oracle, medium, or divination cards such as tarot. Using these tools alleviates the expectation that you will hear what your loved ones have to say to you verbatim. Using these supportive tools will help you feel more confidently connected to spirit. First, ground your energy and surround yourself with protection. Next, invite your spiritual guides to assist you. For example, invite your loved one by name and then draw cards to establish a link and have a conversation with them. It can be most helpful to ask questions of them to begin.

You may also receive messages from loved ones through an exercise known as automatic writing. This is a psychic activity that replaces your own thinking mind with a free flow of channeled words onto paper. Focusing on an activity such as writing or doodling can further remove you from your left-brained or more analytically minded activity in order to allow the words and thoughts of spirit to permeate your mind. The key to automatic writing is quieting the mind so that you can begin writing without stopping for a period of time. During this time, you do not think about what you are writing; just allow the words to flow through you onto the page. Read it when you are finished to spot where the words are no longer yours—those are messages from spirit.

You may choose to add these methods to your psychic development toolbox to strengthen your psychic muscles and feel more confident about your own natural gifts and abilities.

CONSIDER THIS

Though it's ever so subtle and almost barely there, there *is* a space waiting for us all to calm our minds, turn our attention, and feel the presence of spirit, like a light mist of promise and hope falling softly on our skin, which is what it feels like to connect with loved ones and other spirit beings in the afterlife. It is a matter of moving through the mist of this plane of existence to another one with our inner eye activated and heart wide open to experience it. The magical moment when you are able to make a connection with a loved one or other spirit being is often beautiful and moving.

Our departed loved ones don't feel the tremendous loss of separation as we might, because they are no longer functioning under the thumb of the human ego, which is where many of us have convinced ourselves we are separated from our loved ones at death. Those in spirit don't know what the loss of separation feels like, as they are able to be close to those they love. As spirit, they have the capacity to merge with all things and to at once feel the vast expansiveness of the universe. They have just woken up, free from the physical body, so when they find their way back to loved ones left behind, it can be confusing for them to feel sadness, anger, and pain emanating from those loved ones.

Yes, there are those loved ones who linger longer than others, because they have a difficult time accepting their own death. In addition, there are spirits who suddenly "forget" they are dead, a phenomenon I call psychic amnesia. When you feel your loved ones' sadness, what you are typically feeling is their memories of sadness, not the spirit's real emotion. Forgiveness, love, and acceptance are the three opportunities they have for continued healing. They are no longer conscious beings, but as souls they are still evolving into their next lifetime. We never stop having the chance to heal and grow.

Hearing from your loved ones from the other side can be deeply healing and provide closure and reassurance. That said, it's important to know your boundaries. If there are unresolved issues between you and a departed loved one, it may be best to wait until you have had time to sort them out before attempting to make a connection.

Personally, when I connect with spirit, it is an extremely subtle shift—almost so subtle that if I blink or get distracted, it is gone. It requires a tremendous amount of concentration. But once I establish a link, the information just flows. I get images, memories, their personality, and messages. It is as if I suddenly turn my head sideways and see someone walking into the room I have never met before. I don't see them with my physical eyes, I see them with my inner vision. Sometimes I imagine they have been teleported from another place, because if I were actually to see them with my physical eyes, that is how they appear: much like a holographic image from another dimension. I have had lots of fun connecting with my own loved ones over the years and have had so many deeply inspiring experiences.

STORY

Spirits often catch us by surprise, especially our own loved ones. My mom called me one day in recent months and said it was so strange, she hadn't been thinking about her brother who crossed over several years ago, but suddenly she couldn't get him out of her mind. The thoughts of him sort of kept creeping into her mind out of the blue for a few days. There was nothing significant about the timing; it wasn't a birthday or anniversary, and so it was puzzling to her why she was thinking about him so much. Suddenly, she got a phone call from one of her brother's high school friends, inviting my mom to attend his high school reunion and bring some of his artwork to share with their graduating class. She then understood why he was in her mind so frequently.

This example is more than a common occurrence when it comes to spirit connection, and these little synchronicities are often spirit's way of collaborating with us as we are still living. But it's not necessary to sit back and wait for your loved ones to come to you. Relaxing your mind in meditation removes the wait time. In fact, reaching out to them is much like picking up the phone and dialing them. Sometimes they are available, other times they aren't, depending on what they are going through at that particular moment.

It is worth mentioning that when our cherished loved ones are deeply missed, connecting with their spirit may often bring about a grief response. Grief is an emotion, and it's nothing to feel afraid of. However, you'll want to be sure you feel ready to crack your heart open before embarking on this particular meditation exercise. Begin by choosing one or two cherished loved ones or friends with whom you were on good terms when they departed.

Allow twenty to thirty minutes for this meditation. It is advised to find a quiet space where you won't be disrupted.

MEDITATION

When you have found yourself in a comfortable place, close your eyes. In your mind's eye, go to some place in nature that you love or long to be. Focus on the space. Engage all of your senses now. Notice what you feel, what you hear, what you taste, what you smell, and take in the sights of your surroundings. This is your own sanctuary of comfort and support. Your guides may join you here. Your loved ones may also join you to connect.

When you are centered and in your sanctuary, invite your spirit guides to join you here. They will assist in facilitating the connection between you and your loved one. Direct them to bring a loved one from the light who you would like to connect with. Call them to you from the light.

Combine all of your senses now to connect. Imagine, sense, or feel this person sitting right in front of you. What does their voice sound like? What words do they use? What do they smell like? Look like? What are they wearing? What is their mood or attitude? Be with this moment. Don't rush it. You are inviting them into your company.

Feel the love that this person has for you emanating from their being. Allow yourself to embrace them, greet them, or speak to them in whatever way feels appropriate.

See, sense, or feel their love as a pure, warm light. You may choose any color for this light. Allow the color that surrounds them to appear to you. Sense this light surrounding your loved one. It may take a few moments to feel them coming close to you. Breathe and relax.

If you find yourself struggling in any way, invite them to come closer to you. With the assistance of your spiritual guides, you are in charge of facilitating this connection. Be bold. Be clear about what you want this experience to be: you are co-creating it with the abundant help of the spirit world.

Now, feel and visualize your own aura of pure light surrounding yourself. Feel it grow in size as you feel loving energy pouring from your heart center, located in your chest area. In this moment of reunion, bask in the feelings of love and joy you feel toward or receive from your deceased loved one. Allow it to uplift your emotions. Feel gratitude for their presence in your life.

Say what you need to say. It is perfectly acceptable to ask for forgiveness, especially if there was anything left incomplete between you when they were alive. Or you may choose to express your gratitude for their role in your life.

It is now time to invite them to share with you whatever they wish: perhaps a nugget of wisdom, memory, or hobby that was important to them, or it could be guidance or advice on your life path. Whatever they share moves in the space of love and connection. Feel your loved one's peace and love as they permeate your conscious mind and heart.

Allow the tears to flow. You have waited a long time to be reunited with them, and they to you. Tears provide a cleansing release and an avenue for profound healing.

Feel the healing energy of their continued love surrounding you as it heals any grief you may be holding over their passing. It is in the space of connection at this moment you realize you were never parted for good, just for a moment.

Even if you are convinced at this point that you are merely imagining all of this, it's important to continue. Imagination and your inner vision are twin sisters, acting together in collaboration to bring about insights and awareness. As we exercise our imagination "muscle," it gets stronger and stronger. Our imagination is a doorway that grants us access to all higher levels of inner vision. Through practice, inner vision will become more and more real. You'll soon reach the point where the emotional shift you enter into while doing this meditation becomes proof itself that you are in fact having a real experience.

I've found that after doing this meditation, I can feel my loved one around me for many hours afterward and often receive physical signs that verify this. I also feel incredibly energized and spiritually uplifted. After-death contact leaves me with a feeling of peace and joy that sometimes lasts for days.

Helpful Guidance: Out of all the meditations in this book, this is *the* one that requires you to be absolutely certain there will be no interruptions. Be gentle and patient with the process. Making contact with your loved ones can bring a deep emotional release.

FOR YOUR JOURNAL

Take a moment to write down as much as you can recall about who came forward to connect with you: What did they look or feel like? What they were wearing? Were there any other significant details? What was their message to you?

TWENTY
Past Lives Meditation

It is possible to go to a place for the first time and feel in some mysterious way as though you have been there before—or upon meeting someone new, feeling like you have known them your whole life, if not longer. For example, imagine you are on a work trip. You reluctantly agree to attend a party with colleagues that evening. You aren't sure why, but something seems familiar about that moment. It's only a hint, but nevertheless it's there, and it's not the usual feeling of a work party. You are left wondering what happened and why you felt that way. Next, you inadvertently bump into someone. It's embarrassing, but you both politely apologize and in the next few moments, you cannot get over the feeling you have met somewhere before. You ask, "Do I know you?" Three hours pass in a flash as you are swept away into conversation with a familiar feeling, as though you two have known each other forever.

This is the classic example of what happens when we meet someone we've known before or go someplace we've been before, connected to a previous lifetime. It can be our sixth-sense way of connecting with places, people, and events from past lifetimes.

CONSIDER THIS

You were born because, on a spiritual level, you desired complete expression of your spirit and soul through human form. You had previously been in spirit, dancing through the cosmos, experiencing the full expansion of this universe in between lives. You can reconnect to past lives by going beyond that space through the vehicle of your subconscious, where past life memories are stored. Some of us desire the understanding and knowledge of our full story as a soul: where we've been, how we got here, and what we are here to learn. If we're lucky we'll also receive the understanding of what we are here to heal. I believe some of our current lifetime's wounds, relationships, and behaviors stem from lifetimes past. We may have forgotten them upon reincarnation, but they aren't lost to us. We can find them again.

Connecting with your past lives is a psychic experience. Everything you have ever been a part of or ever will be is within your grasp to know and understand. When you do a past life meditation, please go in with the understanding that you have likely had multiple past lives. I believe most of us alive on the planet have had more than one past lifetime, as this planet has been in existence for millions of years. Entire civilizations have come and gone.

When you feel a strong connection to other places and time periods on the planet, it may be an indication of having had a past lifetime. I know I have. I am obsessed with historical fiction, especially of medieval Europe, and am mystified by Egyptian artifacts in museums. I stare at them and something just feels familiar. I love watching movies and TV set in the American Old West. One of my most favorite childhood trips was to Deadwood, South Dakota, and I can still remember to this day feeling oddly like I belonged there, though in a time period long gone. Feelings like these can serve as hints and clues to us about time periods and ages in history in which we might have been alive.

The best strategy for success with the following meditation is to allow your soul to guide you to whatever past life that you need to see in particular at that time. Your soul's innate wisdom will provide the opening for what you need to know. Remember that there are some things you are just not ready to know or see yet, so you don't need to continue in a meditation that shows you things that don't feel right to you. If anything makes you uncomfortable, it's okay to end it, ground yourself, clear your energy, and come back. However, if you allow yourself to stick with it until the end, you afford yourself the gift of doing some incredible healing, and providing closure to traumas that happened to you hundreds of years ago, potentially impacting your current lifetime.

For some reason, people are more likely to discredit a psychic experience that includes a past lifetime than they are ones relating to their current life. After doing years of this work, I believe I have an understanding about why. We have strong sense memories in this lifetime. Something seems more real-world and tangible when we are focusing on the events of this, our current lifetime. When we are connecting with past lifetimes, our sense memories are different. We still have them buried in our subconscious mind, where those memories are held until we are able to access them. However, we have no conscious recollection of those lifetimes, so when a story we are reliving is experienced and those old emotions are felt again, and the time and place become more vivid in our minds and hearts, it is much easier to discredit it as our imagination. The sense memories don't hit us nearly in the same way as what is received through our psychic abilities regarding events and circumstances of this present lifetime.

Our psychic abilities work when we are conscious of amplifying all of our senses, including our sixth sense. People who psychically receive through any of the clairs can beautifully and easily connect to past lifetimes. Be aware that if you are more clairsentient (feeling), you may only experience things in the form of emotional release—feelings of sadness, grief, elation, excitement, bliss, and happiness—that can come surging through you, rather than images or memories (as they would with someone clairvoyant).

Clientss ask me all the time whether what they are experiencing is real or their imagination. When it comes to past life work, it isn't critical to determine whether whatever comes to mind is a symbol, metaphor, true memory, the imagination, or a mixture. Usually, you won't be able to track that lifetime to something real, though there have been spectacular examples of people who received a name, location, and time period and were able to track their own past lives. This is especially common with children, who have such pure, uncluttered souls that allow them to more easily connect with psychic experiences both of this world and the next.

What is the purpose of accessing past lifetimes? This question is answered differently for everyone. Some wish to discover why they have certain habits or behaviors that appear out of the blue and seem difficult to break. Others wish to catalyze healing in a relationship through understanding that relationship's deep history, which often spans lifetimes. Others are just curious. It really doesn't matter what the reason is for you, as long as you understand what you are hoping to gain from exploring here. It can be a magical, life-changing moment to be in the heart of the story of your past lifetime. I believe the goal should be whatever helps us learn about ourselves, and to heal and make better choices.

Past life meditation allows us another way to understand the continuity of the soul which goes on from lifetime to lifetime. Author and psychiatrist Brian L. Weiss shares with us the beauty of the soul's essence, in his book *Miracles Happen: The Transformational Healing Power of Past Life Memories:*

> To see and appreciate the soul of others with whom you are in a relationship is a higher state of awareness. To see only their outer characteristics provides a limited and incomplete perspective. Their current personality, just like their current physical body, is a temporary manifestation. They have had many bodies and many personalities but only one enduring soul,

> only one continuous spiritual essence. See this
> essence and you will see the real person.

This statement reinforces that we access more of our own soul's essence through the knowledge of our past lifetimes. It offers us the opportunity to know our fullest selves.

If you don't experience something profound during this meditation, don't worry. You may continue to have spontaneous flashes of insight in your waking state after the meditation ends, which is sometimes how it happens. Do not for a moment presume you aren't having a past life experience just because you aren't getting anything in the moment. The visions may even come through a dream or daydream. Stay open and patient with the process. Know that the healing works through you whether or not you are clear on what the past life exactly was. Who you were and what happened are secondary to the closure, healing, and release that go along with this meditation.

There is significance in the symbolism used in this particular meditation. The garden portion of the meditation represents a safe haven (just like your own personal sanctuary) and a place of comfort where you can go to rest, should you need a break. I reserve the garden imagery specifically for this meditation, as I feel it provides a particularly special trigger when used in an ongoing manner for these deep subconscious memories to surface.

I also reserve the image of descending a staircase for this particular meditation. Symbolically, the act of descending a staircase leads to deeper levels of concentration, and it also builds anticipation and focused awareness. Your conscious and subconscious mind will learn to respond to this imagery when it is used consistently. One of the best things about repeated meditation for accessing your psychic abilities is that it trains the mind, physical body, and energy body to work in harmony in predictable ways. It's in the space of repetitive ritualistic preparation that creates a clearer opening for psychic insights to surface.

It can be helpful to begin with a reflective exercise: Are there any patterns, beliefs, ailments, relationships, behaviors, or habits you are curious about or suspect as being connected to you from a past lifetime? Is there a specific time period you would like to know whether or not you are connected to? You desire this experience for a reason, and there is definitely something in the present moment that guides you to reveal the path. Each time you do this meditation, you may experience a different lifetime. Allow your soul to guide you where you need to go for today.

Can you lie down for a brief period of time and focus, say 30 to 45 minutes without falling asleep? If not, it may be better to sit either on the floor or on a chair. Knowing how you best relax without falling asleep can help you with this and all other meditations.

MEDITATION

Close your eyes and begin with your breath, slowing the pace of your breathing to one that feels more calming and comfortable. Notice the air flowing in and out of your lungs, and just feel into it for a moment. Breathe in and out, in and out. Each time you breathe out, say to yourself the word "release" as you allow all the tension, concern, and weight of your day move down your grounding cords to be safely transported away from your body.

Tell yourself with each breath out you are growing exponentially more relaxed. Feel all the muscles, tissues, organs, and membranes of your body fully release and relax. With each breath out, allow yourself to go even more deeply into this wonderful flow of calm. Continue breathing for some time. Take your time; this is the relaxation portion of this meditation.

Now with each breath you are releasing, imagine in your mind's eye that you are setting down the heavy weight of the load that is this current lifetime. Bring to the surface any residual cares or concerns that are still lingering. Witness your mind beginning to slow down. With each breath, your thoughts become more difficult to hang on to. They are fading now into the background and disappearing.

Notice with each breath that you are feeling more full and calm and present. Allow yourself to even more deeply relax; your breathing now has achieved ease and a flow that is most comfortable.

Imagine, know, see, and feel yourself walking in a meadow somewhere. We don't need to know where right now. It seems familiar, like a distant memory, a place you've been before. Gently walk yourself through the meadow to a large stone wall. In the wall is a doorway that leads to a hidden garden. Open the door and walk through it.

On the other side of the door is the most enchanting garden you've ever seen. Allow all of your senses to open now—your sense of sight, hearing, smelling, tasting, and touching. Run your fingers along the vegetation filling this space with its beauty and radiance. Allow yourself to explore here, taking it in fully. This is a resting place.

As you walk along further, you notice a beautiful fountain. This fountain is unlike any other. You approach it, and the water pouring from the center seems to glow. You are compelled to touch the water, and as you do so, you feel a surge of healing power streaming upward through your arms, shoulders, areas in your body that need replenishing. Allow a few moments of just experiencing this beautiful healing fountain. Feel it removing the weight of your current life and any residual energies that could hinder your journey today.

Pause, breathe, release, and relax.

When you are finished here, continue walking through the garden and feel the protective, safe atmosphere of this beautiful place. In the distance you see a stone staircase leading downward. Walk to this staircase and with each careful step down, feel yourself moving even deeper into a state of relaxation. When you are ready, open the door and step through to another time and place.

Feel, see, sense, or know where you are: the setting, the landscape, the textures and colors of the space and structures around you. Notice who, if anyone, is around you. Take a moment to smell and touch your surroundings. Bend down, and touch the ground. What does it feel like? Look like? Take a moment to get steady in your body, feel the weight of it, sense its gender.

Breathe, relax, breathe, and relax. Start out on foot and walk yourself around this place in a time before today. Allow the images and the feelings, the knowing, to permeate your mind and your heart. You have been here before.

What is happening around you? Stop, and take it in. Go to your home; who is there? What does it feel like to be there? Enjoy the moments in silence to reconnect to this place. Share a meal with those around you. Notice what kind of food you eat, who you share it with, and their connection to you.

Notice now the intricate details of your surroundings. Explore the area you live in. Allow now an awareness of the significance of this time and place and how this time affected you. What was that life's purpose? What were the lessons you learned? How does it connect to this lifetime?

Allow yourself as long as you wish to explore and become familiar with this time and place, deep in your past. When you feel ready, breathe and release whatever you wish to let go of from that time. It is all a part of your soul's path, but it no longer needs to affect your current life.

Walk now back to the door you came from. Go up the staircase to the garden. Wander through it to the door in the stone wall, back through the meadow, now coming back into your body. Breathe into your body as you feel yourself coming back to the present day and the present time.

Helpful Guidance: The success of a past life meditation relies heavily on having as few current life influences or reminders as possible. Avoid using strong scents or modern-sounding music. I also recommend lying down so that your body can fully relax into it.

FOR YOUR JOURNAL

Write down who you were and any other details from that life-time: the landscape and surroundings, the food, the smells, the people, the vibe, and the lessons your soul learned from that lifetime. How can the person who was you from that lifetime help you now?

TWENTY-ONE
Further Development

You have successfully worked your way through all chapters and meditations for psychic development presented here. By now, you have established the foundational components for successfully tapping into more of your own natural psychic gifts and abilities. Your awareness of what's possible has hopefully expanded. You are seeing, feeling, sensing, and understanding things from a completely different perspective than when you began this book. It is a moment to celebrate. Let me personally congratulate you for making it through, one meditation at a time. But…this is not the end! It's only the beginning.

You should now have a basic working understanding of the range of your own psychic abilities in addition to where there is room for more learning and growth. You are more clear now which of the clairs you most fully embody. You are now clear on the ways in which you receive information and guidance. You hopefully have also developed a sense of awe and curiosity for any areas of psychic connection you are eager to explore in more depth. As psychics, we are always in the process of expanding our gifts. It is a practice that gives back over the course of a lifetime.

You may find your mind buzzing with excitement, eagerness, and a hunger to learn more. You also may choose to pause and integrate for a time the things you've learned up to this point. Allow inspiration to guide the process. There is no right way to proceed from here, just suggestions and guideposts for further development.

First, stock your own library with books on topics that speak to your soul and pique your interest. I generally encourage reaching for books on topics you naturally feel drawn to. Your heart, gut, and soul will lead you to the right resources. And your intuition will become your go-to for re-centering and continued learning. When I glance at my own library, I have one solid book on each topic: meditation, tarot, pendulums, chakras, self-healing techniques, past lives, astrology (actually I have several), mediumship, and the cycles of the moon.

Next, create a list of development areas of interest and prioritize them based on your strongest gifts down to your weakest. The mistake many beginning psychics make is in thinking they'll become good at everything. Unfortunately, this is unrealistic and a recipe for becoming scattered and burned-out. Unveiling the one or two areas you excel at and amplifying those areas is the best way to ensure your own personal success. You can chip away at the list slowly; just be honest with yourself about where your true strengths lie and direct your studies accordingly.

Opening your psychic gifts most often happens over the course of years. However, you don't need to have it all figured out to practice—that's why it's called "practice!" Be bold and offer to practice readings on your family and friends. Some of you will be drawn to experimenting with reading others, and others will enjoy developing for personal growth.

Regardless of how you decide to make use of your abilities, a dedicated psychic and spiritual practice continues the expansion of the gifts you have always naturally had within you. You may choose to repeat the exercises here many times, or at least the meditations that you most enjoyed. This book doesn't need to be a one-time read; you can come back to it repeatedly for continued support and to brush up on your skills. Repeat the chapters that stumped you the first time. Go back over your journal and make notations for areas that call to you for further exploration. Be creative, and keep the door open to what's next.

Continuing the development of your psychic abilities allows you the chance to establish an ongoing relationship with the world of spirit all around you. You strengthen your connection to your highest good. You begin to understand how your energy body functions most optimally for the benefit of your physical, mental, and spiritual health. You are better able to navigate the realm of life's slings and arrows with confidence, because you have tools of awareness and understanding consistently at your fingertips.

You can approach the next steps on your journey with confidence and courage. You have explored all the nooks and crannies of your own gifts, and you may now have more questions than when you began. This is marvelous! Working with a private mentor or signing up for a group class for psychic development are two wonderful ways to continue to refine your psychic development practice.

Bibliography

Andrews, Ted. *Animal Speak*. St. Paul, MN: Llewellyn Worldwide, 2002.

Barnum, Melanie. *The Book of Psychic Symbols: Interpreting Intuitive Messages*. Woodbury, MN: Llewellyn Worldwide, 2012.

Buckland, Raymond. *Buckland's Book of Spirit Communications*. St. Paul, MN: Llewellyn Worldwide, 2004.

Ford, Debbie. *The Dark Side of the Light Chasers: Reclaiming Your Power, Creativity, Brilliance, and Dreams*. New York: Riverhead Books, 2010.

Harwig, Kathryn. *The Intuitive Advantage*. Minneapolis, MN: Spring Press, 2008.

Hay, Louise. *You Can Heal Your Life*. Carlsbad, CA: Hay House, 2007.

Judith, Anodea. *Wheels of Life*: *A User's Guide to the Chakra System*. St. Paul, MN: Llewellyn Worldwide, 1987.

Katz, Debra Lynne. *You Are Psychic: The Art of Clairvoyant Reading and Healing.* Santa Barbara, CA: Living Dreams Press, 2015.

Myss, Carolyn. *The Anatomy of the Spirit: The Seven Stages of Power and Healing.* New York: Harmony, 1996.

Newton, Michael. *Journey of Souls: Case Studies of Life Between Lives.* St. Paul, MN: Llewellyn Worldwide, 1994.

Parkinson, Troy. *Bridge to the Afterlife.* Woodbury, MN: Llewellyn Worldwide, 2009.

Peirce, Penney. *The Intuitive Way: A Definitive Guide to Increasing Your Awareness.* New York: Atria Books, 2009.

Ray, Amit. *Meditation: Insights and Inspirations.* Rishikesh, India: Inner Light Publishers, 2015.

———. *Om Chanting and Meditation.* Rishikesh, India: Inner Light Publishers, 2010.

Roman, Sanaya, and Duane Packer. *Opening to Channel: How to Connect with Your Guide.* Oakland, CA: New World Library, 1993.

Shumsky, Susan G. *Exploring Auras: Cleansing and Strengthening Your Energy Field.* Sydney, Australia: Read How You Want, 2012.

Smith, Gordon. *Intuitive Studies: A Complete Course in Mediumship.* Carlsbad, CA: Hay House, 2012.

Weiss, Brian. *Many Lives, Many Masters: The True Story of a Prominent Psychiatrist, His Young Patient, and the Past Life Therapy that Changed Both Their Lives.* New York: Touchstone, 1988.